In the early eighties I confess
My wife started looking for help to change me. She called Jerry, and he graciously agreed to meet with us. That began a good friendship with Jerry and his lovely and caring wife, Rosie. They live the Christian life and leave the judging of others to God. I'm so glad that Jerry finally has put in print his struggles and how he overcame them through God's love and Rosie's support.

—Jerry Hames, retired lumber inspection supervisor

Jerry is a pioneer in the movement of sexual redemption. His years of faithfulness and passion for the Lord give him credibility in sharing this message. You will be blessed as you read his amazing life story.

—Jason Thompson, executive director, Portland Fellowship

Into a world filled with sexual and spiritual confusion comes an honest story filled with vulnerability and transparency. Jerry invites the reader into his life. This book is also an invitation to our own vulnerability and to better understand our own story and beliefs.

—Dr. James C. Putman, PsyD, psychologist

I sat down to read Jerry's book and couldn't put it down!

I have known Jerry Heacock since we were students together at Western Seminary. I knew of his struggle and eventual victory over homosexuality. But I never appreciated the significance of his victory until I read this book. This is the story of a loving and compassionate God, a loving and supportive wife, and Christians who cared enough to listen, offer counsel, and extend agape love. This book will greatly encourage others who struggle with sexual temptation and sin. Jerry's God-honoring testimony declares powerfully that, through God's grace and enablement, believers can be set free from sin and can experience once again the joy of their salvation.

—Dr. J. Carl Laney, author and professor,
Western Seminary, Portland

Brother Jerry is one of my heroes, for his long years of sacrificial love for his wife and for the courageous way he has overcome abuse, addiction, and same-sex attraction. If you are a Christian struggling with same-sex attraction, you need to read this book today! Here is the simple story of a life lived picking up the cross of Christ, a story told with honesty, humor, boldness, and genuine love.

—Tim Davis, founder and director, Pureheart Ministries

Vulnerable and honest, Jerry has experienced sorrow and loss from sexual sin. This is a real story from one who's experienced real transformation. You'll find hope as you see how Jesus is still making people new.

—Alan Hlavka, lead pastor, Good Shepherd Community Church

It takes courage to let people know the secret things of our lives. Jerry's story gives hope to the thousands of men and women who seek to honor God by not living out of same-sex desires.

—Phil Hobizal, contractor and former director, Portland Fellowship

Jerry and Rosie: A great guy and gal serving a great purpose for an even greater God.

—Martha E. Baker, MA, CCC-SLP, and author and former pastor Donald R. Baker, MRE, DD

Saundra and I have known Jerry and Rosie for twenty years. I have wondered about the secret behind Jerry's innermost joy even through challenging times. I have witnessed his deep love for God, his uncompromising, affectionate, and unconditional love for Rosie, and his endless sacrificial work toward the weak and helpless. In this book Jerry candidly shares how he was transformed by the unfailing love and forgiveness of Christ. This transformational power is available for all who sincerely seek it.

—Kofi Nelson-Owusu, pastor, Portland International Church

I've known Jerry for thirty-five years. This book is a testament to God's faithfulness and Jerry's commitment to a lifetime of growth and maturity—from the inside out.

—Dr. Kurt Free, psychologist

Laren and I have enjoyed friendship with Jerry and Rosie almost half our lives. I remember a dark time in my life when every day was filled with the pain of depression. Jerry was there almost every day to encourage and help, even when I didn't want it. We can hear Jerry in the words of his book. You're reading an account of a faithful man and a faithful woman—a man and a woman who have struggled, and through Christ have won.

—John Sloan, editor

Jerry, from his own life, relates a refreshing message that there is true hope for restoration from homosexual struggles.

—Robert A. Singer, pastor, Cottage Grove Bible Church

Jerry is honest about his own struggle, and he encourages every one of us to freedom with the Friend of sinners. I highly recommend this book.

—Lenny Martin, youth pastor,
Good Shepherd Community Church

Choice, Christ, Change—what a concept! My wife and I have known Jerry and Rosie for twenty-eight years and have observed the reality of Christ's redemptive power in Jerry's life. A good read, recommended.

—Hersh Lange, retired police officer, Portland

Twenty years ago I had the amazing privilege of hearing Jerry's story. It opened my eyes to new understanding about homosexuality. May it open your eyes and make you more like Jesus.

—Jonathan Martin, author and outreach pastor,
Good Shepherd Community Church

I've pondered the reason for Jerry's consistent, bountiful, amazing joy. "Those who have been forgiven much, love much." Jerry's life is a wonderful manifestation of the Father's unconditional love, endless forgiveness, and unmerited grace. I wept as I thought about how many people struggle daily as he did. I pray this book will provide the hope and liberty so many desperately need. Written on these pages is The Answer. His name is Jesus. Truly, "whom the Son sets free is free indeed."

—Kathy Shea, retired administrative assistant

GAY...OR NOT?

One Christian Man's Journey

Jerry Heacock

www.xulonpress.com

Contents

Part I
My First Thirty-Five Years

Part II
My Second Thirty-Five Years

Part III
My Next Thirty-Five Million Years

Dedication

This book is dedicated to Rosie, my wife for forty years.
Thank you for:

Listening to me..............day and night,
Loving me.......................even when I have been so very unlovable,
Laughing with me.........even when it was a struggle to laugh,
Forgiving me ....sacrificially and unconditionally,
Singing with me..............even though you are not a singer,
Praying with me..............in both times of tears and times of rejoicing,
Dreaming with me........when we looked to the future,
Working with me...........especially side by side in ministry,
And so much more.

Rosie, you are my best friend,
*   a lovely, fragrant rose like no other—*
*   for you keep on blooming all year long—*
*   winter, spring, summer, and fall.*

Editor's Preface

*Y*ears ago, when I first knew Jerry and Rosie, I was part of a pastoral team at their church. I knew about Jerry's history with homosexuality and his occupation as a chaplain, but I didn't know him well. Now, having spent the last nine months collaborating as Jerry's editor and author coach, I count myself blessed to be this dear couple's friend. We've toiled over manuscripts, laughed over meals, and wept over each other's stories.

I've had several gay friends through the years, but my acquaintance with Jerry has been the first with someone who has left homosexuality completely behind. Jerry is proof that this transition is possible, though very difficult. I respect more highly than ever the person who battles against unwanted same-sex feelings and behaviors.

Jerry and Rosie consider that a major part of their purpose on earth is to provide help and offer hope to Christians with unwanted same-sex attraction. And together I know they wish this book to speak to you, dear reader, as though you were with them in person, sitting in their living room, conversing with them.

No matter who you are, no matter what you've done, I guarantee you're accepted and loved in the Heacock home. And in their hearts.

Welcome.

Brian Smith, editor and author coach

Foreword

I love a good story.

That's probably why my favorite type of book is the memoir— the story of an ordinary individual who has had some kind of extraordinary experience.

You're holding such a book in your hands. I have known Jerry and Rosie Heacock for over thirty years, and their story is extraordinary. Their dedication to each other through many difficult challenges has been an inspiration to me. And their ministry to hurting individuals has also been consistent through the years. They are the "real thing"— genuine and humble Christians who are making a difference in the lives of others because of their faithfulness to Jesus Christ.

So I'm excited to see the potential for their lives to impact others through this book. The issue of homosexuality is being discussed everywhere, both inside and outside the church. I think it's vitally important for stories like Jerry's to be heard. So often we hear one side of the issue, while other opinions are marginalized and silenced.

Jerry represents and speaks to individuals who have struggled with same-sex feelings but have chosen not to embrace a gay identity. As you will read in this book, the pathway to emotional wholeness is not a simple road; it is filled with detours, roadblocks, and barriers. But, then, the pathway to spiritual maturity is difficult for all Christians, not just those who struggle with same-sex issues. We are all "in process," and Jerry's testimony is clear that, like all of us, he has not yet arrived. But he is well along the pathway in his pursuit of a full and deeply rewarding life.

So read his story and be encouraged. Inspired. Challenged. Ultimately, this book is a powerful witness to the love and grace of

Jesus Christ, who reaches out to all of us in love, offering His wholeness as we surrender the broken places in our lives to Him.

"Now to Him who is able to keep you from stumbling, and to present you faultless before the presence of His glory with exceeding joy, to God our Savior, who alone is wise, be glory and majesty, dominion and power, both now and forever. Amen" (Jude 24-25).

Bob Davies, Executive Director of Exodus International, 1985-2001

Introduction

Personal Words to My Readers

*T*hanks for picking up my book. I take it as a compliment that you would be interested in reading about my life.

Perhaps you are struggling with same-sex attraction in your own life. Or you know someone else who is, and you want to learn more. Or perhaps you are researching this subject. As you already know, this is not an easy subject with which to deal. Some people view homosexuality as being inborn or genetic. Others view it as learned behavior. Some see it as natural and others as very unnatural. Some see it as okay and others see it as sin. Some people believe it is impossible to change one's sexual orientation, while others believe it is possible, though not easy.

I want you to know at the outset that I am not writing this from a scholarly or researched viewpoint, but rather I am writing out of my own life experiences. Many books are already available about homosexuality. Yet I sense a shortage of books written from firsthand experience.

I am seventy years old and have dealt with this issue for six decades! Perhaps starting about forty-four years ago, I began thinking that *if* I ever found freedom from my homosexuality, I would want to write a book about it to help others. During the many years of my deep struggles, I never recall reading one book about someone gaining the victory over same-sex attraction and homosexual behavior. After finding the way to victory and after living on the path of freedom from homosexuality, I have increasingly wanted to write my story. How I painfully recall my seemingly endless and hopeless struggles. Now I want to offer a ray of hope and light to others, so they might be encouraged and not give up prematurely.

I am not proud of my past involvement in the various homosexual behaviors and lifestyle. I am deeply ashamed of it and regret what I did. How I wish it were possible to go back and relive much of my life. Yet I can and will live differently now and in the future, by God's help and grace.

Have you ever felt helpless and hopeless due to homosexuality in your life, or in the life of a friend or relative? You are not alone. Many have felt this way. I know I did; I even wanted to give up on life. Let me assure you that as long as you have life and breath, you can get help and renew your hope.

Consider the following parable about my life:

> The old, neglected upright piano was covered with dust and terribly out of tune. The battered instrument was about to be sold at auction. Two helpers wheeled the squeaky monstrosity up to the front, and the auctioneer eyed it dubiously. If he was fortunate, he would talk some charitable soul into parting with a fiver for it. A curious child reached out and poked at a couple of the ivories, eliciting only sounds of dissonance and sorrow. People shuffled in their seats, waiting for something interesting. Waiting for something else.
>
> Then from nowhere appeared a bearded man carrying a black leather tool bag. He approached the sad, old piano, viewed it from several angles, and then set to work cleaning, polishing and tuning it. After fifteen minutes the man set a chair in front of the keyboard, sat, and began to play. And what emerged was a heavenly melody sweeter than that of any classical composer.
>
> The bearded man then stood and walked from the room. Everyone was stunned, including the auctioneer. Realizing where he was, he swallowed, blinked, and began, "Who'll give me—"

The crowd erupted with bids, each person eagerly trying to outdo the next. Only one could become the proud new owner of this fine instrument.

What changed the old piano's worth? The touch of a master's hand[1]

Yes, 'tis true, my life had become like an abandoned piano, useless for its original purpose, destined for the junk heap. Helpless and hopeless was I. But then my Best Friend surprised me. He heard my cry and hastened to my side. He rescued me from oblivion; He transformed my life, restored me to the instrument He designed me to be. He filled me with unending hope and promised to never leave me, nor forsake me.

All of this and so much more from the touch of my Master's hand. And this can be your story.

I wish it were possible for me to sit down with you, face to face, and share my story. Please try to picture yourself seated in front of me as you read this book. And try to imagine my gestures, my pauses, my tears, my sighs, my laughter, and my joy. For then you will allow my innermost being to speak to the depths of your innermost being.

Accept my threefold invitation to . . .

Come be with me—Presence
Come listen to me—Listening
Come receive my gift of love to you—Love

Most important, my prayer for you is that God will open your eyes to see what He wants you to see, to hear what He is saying to you, to understand the hope God is offering you. By faith, receive God's hope, and you will never regret it.

"Now to Him who is able to do exceedingly abundantly above all that we ask or think, according to the power that works in us, to Him be glory in the church by Christ Jesus to all generations, forever and ever. Amen" (Ephesians 3:20-21).

---

[1] Based on "The Touch of the Master's Hand" by Myra Brooks Welch, in *The Best Loved Poems of the American People*, New York: Doubleday, 1936, 222-223.

I Stand Amazed (1973)

I cannot stay here. But how can I leave at the start of this communion service? O God, I feel so dirty. I am covered with sin and filth. Oh, yes, God, I know You have forgiven me of all my sins. But I just keep on sinning! I ask Your forgiveness, over and over again. And as far as I know . . . and hope . . . You keep on forgiving me. But, God, how can you possibly forgive me for repeatedly sinning, and committing the same sins over and over, and over?

Oh, God, I am not worthy of Your forgiveness. How can You love me? Maybe You forgive me because You "have" to, as You promised. But then You surely cannot love me! I cannot love or accept myself, Lord. So I don't think You can love me.

I am such a wretch. I do not deserve to be in Your presence. And surely I do not deserve to partake of communion. How very wrong for me even to think or assume it is okay for me to take the bread and juice, representing the body and blood of Your Son, Jesus. I cannot do this, I must somehow get out of here! I must try to leave this service as soon as possible!

But then gradually my ears (and my heart) begin to hear the lovely, inviting notes of the hymn being played by the organist: "I Stand Amazed in the Presence." And a huge lump lodges in my throat. And my eyes start filling up with tears. And I begin reflecting on the words of this hymn:

I stand amazed in the presence
Of Jesus the Nazarene,
And wonder how He could love me,
A sinner, condemned, unclean.
How marvelous! How wonderful!
And my song shall ever be:
How marvelous! How wonderful!
Is my Savior's love for me!

As my heart and mind continue interacting with the music and words of this hymn, God melts my heart and invites me to draw closer to Him, and to gaze with wonder and amazement once again at Jesus dying on the cross. Not just for the sins of the world, but also for me, and for all of my sins!

He took my sins and my sorrows,
He made them His very own;
He bore the burden to Calv'ry,
And suffered and died alone.
How marvelous! How wonderful![2]

Soon I begin to believe and to accept His love and forgiveness along with His invitation to draw closer once again. I stay for the rest of the service. I leave feeling renewed hope and assurance of God's love for me.

---

[2] Charles H. Gabriel, "I Stand Amazed in the Presence."

Part I
My First Thirty-Five Years

Chapter 1

Early Years

I will exalt you, O LORD, for you lifted me out of the depths and did not let my enemies gloat over me.

—King David, Psalm 30:1, NIV

Amazing grace! How sweet the sound
That saved a wretch like me!

—John Newton, "Amazing Grace"

The Space Needle may be what first comes to mind, when one thinks of Seattle, Washington. Yet for me, I first think of it as the city where my dad, my brother, and I were born. Our country was in the last year of World War II when I was born on January 8, 1945. My dad worked for Boeing and my mom was a public elementary school teacher. My brother, George, had been born a year and a half before me.

In my baby book, my mom wrote this description of me when I was age two: "There's never been a sweeter baby than he has always been— such a nice disposition (can be quite stubborn at times tho')."

My favorite song was "Jesus Loves Me" and my favorite recreation was eating. Mom wrote this about my second birthday: "Birthday dinner at home with family. . . . After dinner Jerry crawled up on the table and practically finished eating his big sponge cake before he was discovered."

My parents' full names were William Edward Heacock and Edith Vonda (Forster) Heacock. They went by Bill and Vonda. My Grandma Florence Heacock did not work outside the home and my Grandpa William Heacock was a salesman much of his working years. Both lived in Seattle. My mom was born, along with her identical twin sister Vida, in Ochiltree County, Texas, one of eleven children (three boys and eight girls)! Her parents, Jesse and Addie Forster, were kept very busy raising their children. My grandfather was a farmer and a mechanic.

Vida and Vonda, the twins, 1955

My family moved to Eugene, Oregon, when I was one year old. My dad was a jeweler (or "goldsmith," as he preferred) until finally retiring at age ninety. He was gifted and creative, constantly seeking to improve his skills at designing, making, repairing, and selling fine jewelry, as well as training others. In fact my dad was hoping that either my brother or I would want to become a jeweler. Then he could train one of his sons in the trade. My dad was disappointed that neither of us pursued that career.

My mom was an elementary school teacher—full-time for a while, but mostly as a substitute while we were growing up. First grade was her favorite age. She was a gifted teacher and highly sought after. In fact we later learned that teachers would often call my mom first, to see if she was available to fill in for them, before they would call in sick.

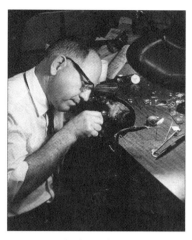

Dad, the goldsmith

My parents took us with them to Sunday school and church from the time I was about three. We attended the First Baptist Church in Eugene. In 1951, when I was in the first grade, I prayed to receive Jesus as my Savior at the end of our church Christmas program. I had heard the gospel for several years and wanted to respond sooner, but was afraid to walk down the long aisle at the altar calls. I thought that was the only way a person could become a Christian. I was baptized at age eleven by our pastor, Dr. Vance Webster.

I have many special memories of both my parents reading stories to us, especially at bedtime. My dad would make up stories that were full of adventure and surprises. He was quite the storyteller!

As a young child, I had problems with scary nightmares. At times I would wake up screaming for help. Often my dad was the one to come check on me. As soon as he was there, I felt safe and protected and at peace again.

My mother had strongly wanted a daughter. Then I came along as her second son. I vaguely remember my mom expressing her wish for a girl when I was very young. I tended to be much closer to my mom than my dad. She was a good listener and encourager. She would confide in me about various matters of concern to her. When I had done something wrong, it was usually my mom who would take my side and defend me. I recall her trying to talk my dad into not being too severe when punishing or spanking me.

When I was twelve, my parents adopted a very cute little two-year-old girl named Collette. Finally we had a girl in the family, and everyone was very happy about that. What fun it was watching her grow up and become a young lady. I regret not having had a closer relationship with her as we grew up. Yet I think the ten-year age difference made that difficult.

Of First Graders and Fish

In my early school years, I felt much closer to the girls than the boys. I felt more comfortable with them and less threatened. I was not interested at all in any sports. This put me at a distance from other boys. My first grade teacher, Glendora Burbank, wrote at least one note to my parents on my report card about this matter: "Jerry tends to spend more time with the girls. He needs to learn to play more with the boys, and I hope he has favorable experiences over the summer with other boys."

First grade

My dad served as a scoutmaster for many years, and he got my brother and me involved as Cub Scouts and later Boy Scouts. I enjoyed these experiences. My dad had strongly hoped that my brother and I would eventually attain the rank of Eagle Scout— the highest one can achieve—but we did not stay in long enough.

Fishing was something else that my brother and I would do with my dad throughout our school years. I was not fond of fishing, but I liked being outdoors with my dad and brother. We would mostly go trout fishing in various lakes and some rivers. The most memorable time I recall and cherish is fishing together in a boat at East Lake in central Oregon. We fished there for several days and we caught about one hundred trout. We had a fun time and came home with lots of *fish tails* and *fish tales*! My dad would give me a hard time when I resisted baiting the hooks with worms. He would say things like, "Don't be a sissy. The worms can't hurt you!" I felt he was making fun of me and putting me down, and I felt rejected. I admired and loved my dad and wanted his approval of me. Sadly, although I now realize that my dad wasn't intentionally rejecting me, the repetition of the experience left a strong, lasting impression on me. I found myself torn between wanting to spend more time together with my dad and brother, yet wanting to avoid fishing trips. My self-image was very fragile in those early years.

I wish I had better understood then what I do now. I missed out by not being willing to let my dad know how I felt. I felt he was rejecting me as a person, rather than simply my actions. *Now I realize there is a big difference between my worth and identity as a person, created in God's image, and anyone's assessment of my actions.*

Thankfully, both my dad and brother kept on encouraging me to go fishing with them, even in my adult years. One time I decided to go deep sea fishing on a charter boat off the Oregon coast. We had a great time together and brought home some large salmon. I was relieved we did not have to bait our hooks with worms.

Another memorable fishing trip with my dad and brother (and a few other relatives) was closer to the end of my dad's life. We rented a large lakeside cabin for a weekend and fished in a lake with lots of stumps poking out of the water. The fishing was okay, but I thoroughly enjoyed being together with each of those men! I believe that experience helped affirm my masculinity and acceptance by men I respected as being very masculine.

Fishing with Rosie's family, 1977

Open-Door Policy

I am glad my parents allowed us to have a variety of pets, espe-cially cats and dogs. My dad was much more of an animal lover than my mom. Our first dog was a beautiful white Samoyed. Then I remember a friendly female cat that we just called Mama Kitty—tiger-striped and always having kittens, it seemed. In later years, I still liked cats, but much preferred dogs.

My parents were hospitable the entire time I was living at home. It seemed we were always having relatives and friends over for a meal or just to visit. My brother and I always knew it was okay to invite our friends over. I guess I caught my love of people from my parents at an early age.

We were the "all-American family" who loved one another and functioned very well in general.

But early on something happened that changed my life drastically.

Chapter 2

School Years

O LORD my God, I called to you for help and you healed me.

—King David, Psalm 30:2, NIV

I once was lost, but now am found;
Was blind, but now I see.

—John Newton, "Amazing Grace"

Before I was even born, I was exposed to good music. While I inhabited my mother's womb, my dad played many classical seventy-eight records, including some of the world-famous soprano opera singer, Lily Pons. So I was predisposed to fine music before even seeing the light of day.

My dad would tell how he took me in to a music store to buy some new records when I was about five. The salesperson turned to me and asked what kind of record I'd like, to which I promptly replied, "A Lily Pons record!" To this day, I like a good operatic soprano voice best of all. In fact, my favorite female singer was Beverly Sills, whom I once heard in person.

I loved hearing people play the piano and organ—especially the piano. I began taking piano lessons in the first grade. My teacher was a young lady named Leann, who lived just down the street and played piano and organ at her church. I took piano lessons for five years, first from Leann, then from two other ladies. My mom told me that she never had to make me practice; instead, she had to tell me to *stop* playing. I tended to keep my feelings to myself. But Mom could usually tell how I was feeling by the way I played the piano.

Around fourth grade I took accordion lessons and thought it was fun. But I was using a full-size accordion, which was heavy and hard for me to handle. So I stopped.

Next I played an alto saxophone for about four years in the school bands. I did fairly well and even played with the high school band while only in the sixth grade! In about the ninth grade I switched to cornet and stuck with it through high school and in the marching band for one or two years in college. I did not like the football games all that much, but I had fun playing in the marching band.

I was sometimes frustrated that I could only play *one* instrument at a time. So I got creative and sometimes played the piano with my right hand and my cornet with my left.

Although I had practiced and learned numerous classical pieces on the piano, I did not play them much after stopping piano lessons. Instead, I would play lots of hymns, songs from Broadway musicals, and other popular songs. I delighted in friends gathered around the piano, singing with me. That's still true to this day.

What peace, joy, and creative delight I've often found in playing the piano, even when serving four years in the Army. One of the first things I look for when I'm in a new home is a piano. And when I find one, away I go!

Music wasn't the only area in which I excelled. Getting the best grades possible was always important to me. I was no genius, nor was I a dummy. I enjoyed studying and learning. But I think my main motivation was to feel better about myself and to gain the respect of my peers. I knew that those who excelled in athletics were respected and admired, but I was not athletic. So I worked hard and got mostly A's and Bs up through college. In my mind, anything less than an A was equivalent to flunking the class. I was often jealous of my brother, George, who could do well in school without having to study much. He just had more natural "smarts" than me, it seemed, especially in senior high and college.

I envied my brother's ability to read so much and so well. I loved to read also, but found it more difficult to concentrate for long. My mind would often wander, sometimes veering off into sexual thoughts and fantasies.

My brother usually seemed to have a much closer relationship with my dad than I did, so I was jealous of George for this as well.

Sex: My Introduction and Obsession

When I was growing up, most parents did not talk with their kids about sex. My parents were no exception. I don't recall them ever talking with me about sex until I was in ninth or tenth grade. Then it was only my mother, who spoke with me briefly and had me talk with our family doctor.

The summer of 1954, after third grade, when I was nine, something happened that changed my life for the worse. I was camped outside in a pup tent with a neighbor boy who was about two years older. He reached inside my sleeping bag and began fondling me. I did not understand why he was doing this. Then he took my hand and put it on him and encouraged me to fondle him. This seemed new and strange to me, but also somewhat exciting. I felt that he really liked me, and this was the way he was showing it. I never told my parents or anyone else about this. It was our secret. This experience seemed to quickly and prematurely awaken my interest in sex, but instead of with girls, it was with boys.

This neighbor boy and I continued over the next year having various sexual encounters with each other. Then we moved away, so it stopped. Looking back, I wish I had talked with my parents about what was happening. But guilt and embarrassment kept me from it.

When I was in about the ninth grade, this same neighbor boy came to our home for a visit. We were changing clothes and the next thing I knew we were sitting on the edge of the bed with our pants down, fondling each other. My mom walked in and saw us, then quickly left in shock and embarrassment, not knowing what to say. My parents must have talked it over. They sent me to talk with our family doctor. He asked me some questions and gave me a booklet on the bare basics of human sexuality, expecting that to help me. It did not. I think he must have thought this was just a passing phase and that I needed more information about "normal" sex. I was not interested in sexual contact with girls, but rather with boys my age.

In junior high and much more in senior high school, I experienced a strong sexual attraction to other boys. My thoughts and dreams about this became obsessive and consuming. As far as I knew, others were not aware of this attraction. In fact, I was extremely afraid of anyone else knowing about it. I did everything I could to keep it hidden. This was such a sensitive subject, I did not feel comfortable talking with anyone about this problem before I reached college.

Masturbation became a major problem for me in my teenage years. I was too scared to seek sexual contacts with other boys, for fear of ridicule and rejection. I sensed that masturbation was wrong, yet it seemed okay in some ways, since it did not involve any other person. I entered into a vicious cycle of lusting after various boys, then masturbating, then lusting more and more. My hormones seemed to be working overtime, and masturbating became my main outlet, both physically and emotionally.

Sports was never my thing in school. Yet I was jealous of many boys who were athletes. They were often popular and seemed very masculine to me. I did not see myself as being very masculine, so I found myself often attracted to some of them sexually.

By the way, in about the sixth grade I played on the basketball team in our small grade school and found it somewhat fun. I was not very good at it, but I enjoyed the interaction with the team. This is the main, but not only, positive memory I have of taking part in sports activities while growing up.

Summer of 1957

My first major summer job came in 1957, after sixth grade. I went by car with my Aunt Ellen, Uncle Jac, and my brother, George, to Ochiltree County in the Texas panhandle, near where my mom was born. We spent the summer working on a large grain farm that was owned and run by our distant, elderly cousins, "Shorty" (Allan) and Nora Dennison. They grew many kinds of grain, especially wheat, but also barley, oats, maize, and others.

That summer was a stretching experience for me, transforming me from city boy to country boy. Uncle Jac wrote my parents: "He's very good at handling the tractor." Not too bad for this city boy at age twelve! I loved the farm.

There were many reasons why this experience was significant to me. It provided the chance to mature faster, being far from home for the first time—away from my parents and friends. Also I gained a broader understanding and appreciation for a farmer's life, with all its uncertainties and challenges, as well as an understanding of the value of teamwork. Finally, I developed memorable insights into the vastness and variety of our country.

Near the end of that summer, Uncle Jac wrote to my parents about my brother and me: "Don't think either of their vacations is being made miserable. Far as I can see, they are having a fine time and will arrive home tanned and hale and hearty and drawling like Texans!"

I went back alone four years later, at age sixteen, and worked on the same farm. By then I was old enough to drive a car, not just a tractor in the fields. Without the company of my aunt, uncle, or brother, that summer I developed more maturity and self-confidence. I did *not* return home with a strong desire to become a farmer. Instead I came back home with numerous bottles of Dr. Pepper. I first tasted it there in Texas and loved it. That flavor of soda pop had not yet been introduced in Oregon.

Collette, me, George, 1957

Spiritual Development

From almost my earliest memories I've always had an interest in spiritual matters. No doubt this was in part due to being raised in a

Christian home, hearing my parents pray over meals, at bedtime, and at various other times. I also attended Sunday school and worship services weekly, as well as midweek services. I developed early a growing hunger to learn more about God and His Word, as well as how God wants us to serve Him.

During my grade school years I had the privilege of hearing a variety of missionaries speak. I began to feel a compelling desire to become a missionary. Increasingly I felt burdened to share the good news of Jesus Christ with people who had never heard or understood the gospel message. I remember praying for various missionaries as a young child. In fact, I was only in the first grade when my church sent out Don and Faye Smith to South Africa. I have wonderful memories of praying for them and getting updates on their ministry.

How very thankful I am that God was cultivating my heart at an early age to love Him and to love other people.

Sadly, the enemy of my soul also began working on me from my early youth, seeking to pull me away from God and to tempt me with worldly pleasures—most specifically through sexual sin. Satan was deceiving me, convincing me that I knew best what I needed. Also, I think he led me to believe that I was free to think whatever I wanted, including sexual lusting and fantasies, as long as I did not act on them. Surely it wouldn't hurt anyone if I kept these inside.

I had a distorted idea of what was and was not appropriate to discuss with God. In particular, it seemed inappropriate to talk with God regarding anything about sex. None of the important people in my life spoke about sex. Hence, I felt anything to do with sex was private and not to be discussed, especially with God. That thinking seems so strange to me now. Now I know that God is the One who created us as sexual beings, and He has specific, wonderful purposes for it, within the boundaries of marriage. I wish I had felt open to talk freely with God about sex when I was young—especially about my sexual temptations.

Habla Deutsch?

I began learning Spanish in ninth grade. It came fairly easily to me and I enjoyed it. While I continued Spanish class in tenth grade, I also took a biology class from Herr Holton, the popular German teacher. I was not strongly interested in science, but Herr Holton made learning biology easier and fun. I thought, *If he can make biology fun, then it would be fun to have him as a German teacher.* So my junior year I signed up for first-year German, along with third-year Spanish. It got a bit confusing at times. I would mix up some of the grammar rules, word order, and pronunciation of the two languages. At times, I'd speak Spanish with a German accent or vice-versa.

Finally, in my last year of high school I dropped Spanish and took only second-year German. What a relief to be able to concentrate on one language at a time.

I'll never forget my first day in German class. When all of us students were seated, Herr Holton began with something like: *"Guten tag. Ich heisse Herr Holton, und wie heissen Sie?"* Almost that whole class period was conducted in German, though none of us knew the language. He was giving us a jumpstart and an immediate feel for the language. That was a wonderful way to help us jump right in to learning German. Instead of starting off reciting grammar rules, he assumed we could start understanding and speaking it from day one. He was right!

German quickly became my favorite subject. During my senior year I knew I wanted to major in German in college. In fact, I wanted to become a high school German teacher, and maybe eventually teach it in college.

I did major in German at the University of Oregon in my hometown, Eugene. I took all the required classes to become a German teacher in high school, and even did my student teaching requirement under Herr Holton at my old high school, North Eugene High.

Obsession Comes of Age

In senior high school I only dated a few girls I felt very comfortable with due to common interests, such as foreign language, music, or church activities. I considered the girls I dated as "sisters" in some ways. I was surely not thinking of them in any sexual way. I do not remember going to any of our high school dances. Our church frowned upon dancing. Also, I did not have much confidence that I could do well at a dance.

During senior high school I was becoming increasingly obsessed with sexual lusting and thoughts towards other boys. Naturally I was more drawn to those who were good-looking, athletic, and popular, since I felt I was none of those. These homosexual desires plagued me day and night. I found it more and more difficult to concentrate on my studies, as these thoughts kept intruding. They invaded my dreams as well. The level of confusion, guilt, and shame was difficult to handle. At least I wasn't acting on them, I rationalized; I was keeping them in my head. And at least I wasn't having sex with girls. This was more commonly spoken of as bad and sinful in my church upbringing. Very little mention was ever made about homosexuality before I got into college.

I hoped and believed that when I got into college these desires for my same sex would gradually disappear, because I fully expected to meet the right girl and get married. *Someday...*

Chapter 3

College Years

O Lord, you brought me up from the grave; you spared me from going down into the pit.

—King David, Psalm 30:3, NIV

'Twas grace that taught my heart to fear,
And grace my fears relieved;

—John Newton, "Amazing Grace"

I graduated high school in 1963. That fall I moved into one of the men's dormitories at the University of Oregon (home of the Ducks) in my hometown of Eugene to begin my college studies, majoring in German. I don't remember much about that first year. I'm sure I struggled with many same-sex thoughts, but I don't remember acting on them. I found it difficult to concentrate on my studies with all that was going on in the dormitory. So it was better to live at home for my second year in college. My parents were glad to have me home.

That year we housed a college student named Jim from Taiwan. He was shy at first, but before long he relaxed as part of our household. He and I shared a bedroom. I'm thankful that I was not sexually attracted to him.

My family also became a "friendship family" to various students from other countries. That's how I met Werner from West Germany. He persuaded me to go to Germany with him for the next year and helped me with applying to his university in Bonn. Near the end of that year, he decided to stay another year at University of Oregon. I was disappointed, but he gave me his mother's contact information, so I could visit her. He also gave me the name of his girlfriend, who attended University of Bonn, and she helped arrange housing for me.

I'm actually rather vague on when during my first two college years I started going beyond thoughts and fantasies in my sexual acting out with men. I know that I experienced more and more one-time, anonymous sexual encounters as each college year progressed. But in my mind, this acting out was in many ways a continuation of my experience as a child with the neighbor boy, so when I "started" as an adult doesn't seem that significant to me.

Bon Voyage

On Sunday, September 19, 1965, various friends stopped by to say good-bye and wish me well. The next day my whole family left Eugene to take me to catch the train in Vancouver, BC. On Wednesday I boarded my first Pullman car and was pleased with the accommodations. But I hated saying my final good-bye to my family. I wouldn't see them again for almost a year.

After four days by rail across Canada, I arrived in New York, where I visited my Great Aunt Helen—quite alert and smart at age eighty-seven! I took in many New York sites, such as the World's Fair, the Metropolitan Art Museum, Tiffany's, the Rockefeller Center, the Empire State Building, the Stock Exchange, the Statue of Liberty, and much more.

I visited Washington, DC, and saw the US Capitol building, the Supreme Court, the Library of Congress, the Washington Monument, the Lincoln Memorial, Arlington Cemetery, and the White House, among other sites.

One night while staying at the YMCA, I went swimming in their indoor pool. To my surprise it was *nude swimming* (men only). So I swam in the nude, which seemed very unusual. A man swam by me underwater and touched me sexually. Then he spoke with me and realized I may be interested in him. We agreed upon a time and place to meet later, but he never showed up. I am thankful he did not. This was a vivid reminder of the potential risks and dangers of involvement with strangers.

On October 1, I boarded the largest German passenger ship, the *Bremen*, and began the delightful one-week voyage. I was happy to share a cabin with a German roommate.

On the *Bremen,* **1965**

Soon after arriving, I traveled to Bonn, then the capital of West Germany, where I would be a student at the University of Bonn. I met Edith, Werner's girlfriend. Thankfully she had found a room for me to rent in a nearby town.

Before long, I went to meet Werner's mom in Hilden, near Duesseldorf. She was kind and hospitable. In fact, several months later she told me, "If your parents were not still alive, I would like to adopt you." *She created a home away from home for me.*

A German Revelation

Within a month I was feeling homesick and thought I might not stay in Germany. How could I possibly be wanting to return home? This was a dream come true. I wanted to become a German language teacher. What better place to improve my German fluency than here? Why did I want to go back home?

For one thing, this was my first time living in a foreign country. The culture and language differences created difficulties. I hardly knew anyone, and I had trouble getting around in this unfamiliar place. Also, my initial living situation didn't help. It was some distance from the university, and I commuted by bus. It was a large, older home that rented out rooms. We shared bathrooms. Each room had a coal-burning stove to heat it, and I had to pay for each brick of coal I used. On my limited budget my room would get rather cold, and I found it hard to concentrate on my studies.

I decided to ask God to show me clearly whether He wanted me to stay or go home. I suddenly had a sobering thought: *If God reveals His will to me, will I simply add this to my list of options, or will I surrender fully to His will and obey it?* In fact, I sensed that God was clearly asking me that question, and I was to give Him my decision before He would reveal His will.

God, that's not fair! I protested. *You mean if You tell me to stay here in Germany, that's what I must do?* And I knew His answer was a firm *yes*.

I hesitated, considering the ramifications. Then, with a deep breath, I asked God to show me His will clearly and promised that I would do it.

How God would reveal His will to me, I was not sure. So I took my German New Testament and opened randomly to a passage and began reading these words: *"Ich will zu diesem Volk in Fremdsprachen reden"* (1 Corinthians 14:21). Wow! I could hardly believe what I had just read. It was like God's handwriting on the wall addressed to me. A rough translation is: "I want to speak to these people in foreign languages." It was as if God was reminding me of the primary reason I had come to Germany—namely, to improve my German and become fluent.

I should have been rejoicing that now I clearly knew God wanted me to stay. Yet I had been secretly hoping He would give me His stamp of approval to go home. Now I had to stay and face the challenges, the loneliness, the homesickness, and the strange culture.

I waited and prayed for God's help. Within a few weeks I was invited to live in a coed dormitory within easy walking distance of the university. I had been on a waiting list, and they wanted another American male student with them.

I moved in and began making new friends readily. My fun and friendly roommate was Dieter, a math major. Dieter was good-humored and patient with me. Often in the mornings he'd tell me I woke him up speaking or singing German in my sleep! Once I'd begun thinking and dreaming in German, I knew I had "crossed the language barrier" and was becoming fluent.

My classes were difficult at first, but gradually got easier. Fortunately I found a young lady who tutored me for my most difficult class—Goethe's *Faust II,* with which even the German students had trouble—at no charge!

What a joy to spend my first Christmas in Germany. I missed my family, but I was having fun learning the ways they celebrated there. I was invited to the home of Werner's mom. After supper on Christmas Eve we all went to church together, then came back and decorated the tree. Including real candles! We sang Christmas songs, then took turns, each opening one present at a time.

At other times I'd visit another of my friends' mother, whom I called Tante Martha, in a small town near Stuttgart. She loved music and was familiar with many classical works, including operas. She introduced me to *Fidelio,* Beethoven's only opera, and it quickly became and remains my favorite opera. I love both the music and the story.

One day in class I sat next to a lovely German lady named Ursula. I liked her right away and we had some fun dates. I recall going to meet her family. Usually I called her by her nickname "Uschi." On May 25, 1966, I wrote a poem about her in German, modeled after a famous poem with the same title by Johann Wolfgang von Goethe.

Gefunden

Ich ging in die Vorlesung
So fuer mich hin,
Den Professor zu hoeren,
Das war mein Sinn.

Gerade neben mir
Sass ein schoen's Maedchen;
Ich hoerte dem Professor zu,
Aber zu konzentrieren
War schwer—ein bisschen!

Haette ich etwas nicht verstanden
Dann fragte ich sie,
Zwar nach Daten und Namen-
Um ihre Liebe fragte ich nie!

Ich glaubte im Herzen,
Ich haette sie gerne.
Ihre schoenen Augen
Leuchten wie die Sterne!

Ich stellte ihr die Frage:
"Moechten Sie in der Mensa esssen?"
Sie antwortete: "Aber gerne."
Dann haben wir dort gegessen!

—Jerry *("Der junge Goethe")* Heacock
Bonn, den 25. Mai, 1966
Die Bundesrepublik Deutschland
(West Germany)

The following is an English summary of the poem:

> One day in class at the University of Bonn, I noticed a
> lovely young lady next to me. Of course, I found it dif-
> ficult to listen to the professor! If there was something
> the professor said in German that was unclear to me, I
> only asked her the basics of what he said—regarding
> her love I did not inquire. I thought my heart was
> telling me that I surely liked her—her eyes shone like
> the stars. Finally I asked her if she'd join me for lunch.
> She said, "Gladly," so we ate together!

She had stronger romantic interest in me than I did in her. I enjoyed
her as a good friend, yet I think she hoped it would develop into something longer lasting.

I was privileged to make friends with many international students
from such countries as England, France, Austria, the Netherlands, Italy,

42

Tunisia, Morocco, and Australia. This certainly broadened my outlook on the world, and I became familiar with various languages and customs.

During my two semesters at the University of Bonn, I continued to struggle internally with same-sex attractions. I had a few anonymous sexual encounters with other men, but mostly I wrestled with my thoughts and feelings. I continued to have lustful fantasies toward young men I found attractive. Perhaps one reason I seldom acted out was fear of ridicule and rejection if others found out. Another reason may have been that my consuming passion for learning everything I could about the German language and culture dominated my time and energy.

German wanna-be, 1966

Between semesters I used my break to travel in West Germany, Austria, Italy, and Switzerland, taking in numerous historic sites. When I got back to Bonn, I was ready to dive into my studies again.

My cousin put me in touch with a family in West Berlin, and in June I stayed for one week with them and visited both East and West Berlin. What a sharp contrast. The West was beautiful and thriving and truly a world-class city; the East side still had lots of ruins left from World War II. The Berlin Wall had been built just a few years prior. When I asked an elderly East Berlin man what he thought of life there, he said, "You're an American. You know what freedom is like. We did too at one time." My heart ached over the loss of this people's freedom.

When the second semester was completed, in mid-July, I would have loved to stay longer in Germany. But the US military draft board said I would have to finish college in one more year or lose my college deferment. So I decided it best to return home. Who could have imagined the huge change? I went from being so homesick the previous fall to wanting to stay in Germany.

In late summer I flew from Luxemburg to New York City on Icelandic Airlines, which took about twenty-five hours. When I arrived in New York, the airlines had gone on strike, so I got home to Oregon by bus in about three or four days.

Once a Duck . . .

Thankfully I was able to move into His House—a Christian men's co-op in its first year on the University of Oregon campus, housing about fourteen men. We shared expenses and chores and cooking dinners for everyone. Many of us were active in Campus Crusade for Christ. In fact many of us went to their Arrowhead Springs, California, headquarters for spring break. We learned much about growing in our faith and witnessing to others.

My senior year in college was filled with many good things. And also some bad things. My struggles with same-sex attraction intensified. I lived in constant fear that someone would find out and expose me. I had anonymous sexual encounters with various men whom I'd usually discover in public restrooms or parks. I frequently prayed and asked God to *change* me and take away those strong attractions.

Dave, one of my housemates, was very kind to me and would invite me to visit his family in Portland. I decided to take the risk and confide in him. I told him of my homosexual struggles and he listened, sought to encourage me, and prayed with me. I did better for a while, then fell back into the old habits again. Even when I was not acting outwardly on my desire, I was struggling with my thoughts and feelings and fantasies.

I recall later that year confiding in one of the Campus Crusade for Christ staff men. He prayed for me but added that he felt it was likely just a passing phase.

One of the best things that happened to me in my last year of college was meeting the first of two Rosies in my life. I first met Rosie in a German class. She was everything I thought I'd want in a future wife—a young lady of strong Christian faith, petite, blue eyes, blonde, and vivacious. She was also majoring in German and had a lovely soprano voice. I dated her most of my senior year. In May 1967, I proposed marriage to her.

She said no.

She placed the fault on herself, telling me she did not feel ready yet for marriage. *I was surprised and devastated.* To ease my pain, I went out with a friend and got drunk. It did not help.

Rosie graduated in June and left Eugene. I had to take classes in the summer in order to graduate. I had already completed all my required classes for my major, so I was able to take whatever classes I wanted! What fun to take private piano lessons for credit from a music professor.

Finally I graduated with my Bachelor of arts degree on September 1, 1967, with a major in German. Upon graduation, my military draft deferment ended and I knew I could be drafted at any time.

The Night Before Graduation

I had finally completed my classes and was ready to take part in the September graduation ceremony. My brother, George, was in town for this joyful milestone. We decided to go out for the evening to celebrate. George drove us several places and we had a variety of alcoholic beverages. We started off with beer, then progressed to hard liquor. I was accustomed to beer, having spent the previous year in Germany. I had a sense of how much beer I could handle, but I was not nearly as familiar with the more rapid effects of hard liquor. I got very drunk.

When I got home late, I went straight to bed. Yet I could not sleep. Instead I began thinking about several young men who lived in the neighborhood. I had noticed them many times but had never spoken with them. I had often lusted after them in my thoughts.

Before long I decided to go to their homes and try to connect with one of them. I crawled out my bedroom window, hoping I would not awaken my family. I went to one house down the street where one of the young men lived. There were no lights on. I entered through the unlocked back door and slowly walked into the house, looking for the young man's bedroom. I heard someone stirring, became suddenly afraid, and left quickly.

Next I tried to enter the house of another young man, which was directly across the street from my parents' home. The back door and garage door were locked, but I crawled into the garage through a window. I tried to enter the house, but the inside door was locked. I heard someone coming, so I quickly hid behind a car. When the person entered the garage, I panicked, *flew* out the window, and began running down the street. The young man I had been looking for began chasing me with a baseball bat. He caught up and hit my hand very hard. I was scared beyond words. He made me return to their home. His parents, thinking I had tried to burglarize their home, called the police and made me wait.

When the policeman arrived, he began questioning me. I answered him honestly, though it was not easy. I said that I had been struggling with homosexuality for numerous years and was trying to overcome it, but unsuccessfully. I was sexually attracted to the young man. I told the officer and the family that I had been drinking that night and was not in my right mind.

I was deathly afraid that my parents might find out, so I begged the family not to say anything to them. They offered not to press charges if I would meet with their pastor. I readily agreed.

I met with their pastor within the next week or two and shared my homosexual struggle with him. He was very kind and listened and prayed for me. Then he gave me a booklet to read dealing with speaking in tongues, which he believed might be helpful. I read it over at home and spoke with the pastor once more, as requested, but nothing seemed to change for me. The intense struggle continued.

That experience was both extremely frightening and sobering to me. It helped me understand more clearly the reality of losing my inhibitions when under the influence of alcohol. I knew I would never have had the guts to do what I did had I been sober.

I never told my parents or anyone else about what had happened. And the neighbor family kept their word and never told my parents.

Now I can't help but wonder if it may have speeded up my process of healing and change if they had pressed charges or told my parents.

There were other times before and after this incident when I could have gotten in trouble with the law, but that never happened. I believe God spared me from it.

Chapter 4

Army Years

Sing to the LORD, you saints of his; praise his holy name.

—King David, Psalm 30:4, NIV

How precious did that grace appear
The hour I first believed.

—John Newton, "Amazing Grace"

As I mentioned earlier, I visited both West and East Berlin in the early summer of 1966. The sharp contrast between the two sides of Berlin, divided by the Berlin Wall, was unforgettable. What I observed and what I heard from the West and East Berliners helped me more deeply appreciate all the freedoms we have in the US. I believe my Berlin experience greatly strengthened my love for the USA and played a significant role in my willingness to serve in the military.

I served from October 30, 1967, to August 12, 1971. I chose to enlist for four years instead of waiting to be drafted. I had also taken tests with the Air Force and was approved for officer training. However, they had no openings right then for using my German. Hence, I decided to go with the Army, as they "assured" me of being able to use my German.

I had two months to prepare and imagine what my army time might hold. Over several October days immediately preceding my entering the Army I wrote the following:

Sentiments Upon Entering the US Army

To be honest, my thoughts are not all clear and well organized.

Will I like it or not?

Will I be placed where I can use my German or not?

Will I experience victory or defeat in my own life?

Will the Army and country I serve experience victory or defeat in Vietnam and around the world?

At last, will I return home alive or dead?

Would it not be wonderful to know all the answers to these questions right now?

The answer from God is strongly NO! For it is written the just shall *live by faith!*

I praise God for the privilege of knowing and having a personal relationship with the One who knows the answers to all my past, present, and future questions.

This is my earnest prayer, O God:

May Your fullness within me be seen,

In all its vastness and not through a screen.

Father, God—too often I hinder Your image from being clearly seen by others, because my selfish desires and interests form a screen as it were.

Search me God, and know my heart and thoughts. If You want me to change something in my life, make it known to me.

Thank You God that it is *not* my talents or efforts which are most pleasing to You, but rather simply my *willingness* for you to give me the "desire and power" (see Philippians 2:13) to do Your will.

I must confess I do not always have this *willingness* even, so I just trust You also for this.

Thank You, God, for Your promise to equip completely all of Your soldiers. As the apostle Paul wrote in his letter to the Ephesians (see Ephesians 6:10-18), You promise to equip us with six strategic pieces of armor:

When a person places his trust in You, he receives the first three: (1) "loins girt about with truth," (2) "the breastplate of righteousness," and (3) "feet shod with the preparation of the gospel of peace."

Then as a person follows You in his Christian life, he takes up: (1) the shield of faith, (2) the helmet of salvation (to guard his mind and give assurance of salvation), and (3) the sword of the Spirit (which is the Bible).

Father God, though I shall be a soldier for the United States Army, I shall also be a soldier for Jesus Christ. And You, O God, will always be my Highest Commanding Officer and receive my utmost loyalty.

Amen.

Jerry W. Heacock

Basic Hell

At first I was sent to Fort Ord, California, for my three months of basic training (November through January). What a welcome relief to get a three-week Christmas break in the middle of basic training, which was both physically and psychologically demanding.

What a rude awakening as I began my Army training! That was the first time in my life when I felt I had no will or choices of my own. We were told when, where, and how to do everything, but seldom why. We were told when to eat, when to sleep, when to march, when to go to classes, when to clean, disassemble, and reassemble our rifles, when to do pushups, when to speak, and when to be silent. I kept wanting to ask why. But that was not allowed. "Just follow orders. Do what you are told. Don't ask any questions."

One of the main things I had great difficulty accepting was the emphasis upon learning to kill the enemies in combat. I had never been a fighter and had seldom used a gun. I never much enjoyed shooting .22 rifles at targets with my dad and brother. I recall at times the drill sergeant would have us fix bayonets on our rifles and do thrusting movements while shouting, "Kill! Kill!" That was contrary to my nature— something I hoped I would never have to do. At the same time I tried to pay close attention and learn as much as possible, realizing my life and the lives of others might depend upon my actions. We could be sent to Vietnam where the conflict was then at a high level.

During my basic training I was tempted much, struggling with lustful thoughts toward other soldiers, yet I never acted upon them. Nor do I think anyone knew about my same-sex attractions.

Since I have always been musical and liked songs, I enjoyed some of the short ditties that we sang as we were marching. For example, "They say that in the Army the chicken's mighty fine; a leg rolled off the table and started marking time." Or, "They say that in the Army the coffee's mighty fine; it's good for cuts and bruises and tastes like iodine." Then we would often end with "Gee, Ma, I wanna go, gee, Ma, I wanna go, gee, Ma, I wanna go home."

Basic training ended with an outdoor graduation ceremony. My parents lived too far away to attend. But Aunt Nellie and Uncle Bob, who lived nearby, came and encouraged me with their presence and their words.

Thwarted by the Truth

I was transferred to Fort Devens, Massachusetts, for about five weeks in early 1968. This was headquarters of the Army Security Agency, where I was processed for a security clearance. We were given mundane, routine chores to pass the time while waiting—sweeping and mopping floors and cleaning bathrooms over and over again. Also, we spent hour after hour on KP (kitchen patrol) duty setting up tables, peeling potatoes, and the like.

The highlight of my time there was an overnight stay in Boston. I attended a performance of Haydn's oratorio, "The Creation." Beverly Sills sang the lead soprano solo part. I had never heard of her before and was mesmerized with her angelic voice. I had the privilege of meeting her and thanking her personally. From that time to the present I have considered her my favorite opera singer.

The process of getting security clearance required much patience as I was questioned by various army personnel. An army psychiatrist asked me if I'd ever gone for counseling. I answered yes, and he asked me the reason. I told him honestly that I was dealing with homosexuality and wanted help to change and be free of it. Near the end of my time at Fort Devens I got word that I was not approved for security clearance.

This was surprising and devastating to me. I am almost positive it was because I told them about my same-sex attractions. Otherwise I had a totally clean record.

I was given several other choices of fields for training, and I chose quartermaster school. Soon I got orders for three months of quartermaster school at Fort Lee, Virginia. I recall feeling discouraged and lonely at times. I found some help and encouragement in reading my pocket New Testament late at night with the help of a small flashlight, so as not to awaken other men in the barracks. I wish I had been more open about my faith with my fellow soldiers.

I also recall the lack of privacy in the barracks restrooms. There were no dividers between the toilets. It felt rather uncomfortable to me.

A very special blessing during that spring at Fort Lee was being promoted twice, first to Specialist Fourth Class, then to Specialist Fifth Class—after only seven months in the Army. I remained this rank, as a noncommissioned officer, for the remainder of my service.

Near the start of my training at Fort Lee I applied to enter Officer Candidate School (OCS). I gave the paperwork to the company First Sergeant to submit. I asked him at the end of my training why I had not heard anything about my request for OCS. He told me he had held on to the application! Needless to say, I was surprised and upset.

I quickly forgot my anger and discouragement, however, when I received my orders *to be transferred to West Germany, my first choice of anywhere in the world to serve.* (I was also relieved to avoid Vietnam.) I would like to think that the army took notice of my degree and fluency in German, but that did not appear to be the reason. Out of our class of fifty men, the orders were decided alphabetically by last name. About the first ten were sent to Vietnam, the last ten were sent to Korea, and those in the middle were sent to Germany. *Was I ever glad my last name started with H.* I strongly believe God was involved in seeing that I returned to Germany, even though it appeared to be by chance.

I arrived in June, settled in, and began working as a Special Equipment Repair Parts Specialist. I was then sent for a couple of weeks of special training at the Seventh US Army Noncommissioned Officers' Academy. While there, we were required to get two haircuts each week, and I remember many nights sleeping on the floor in my sleeping bag to save time making my bed perfectly in the morning.

I'm in the Army now! Germany, 1968

Help! I Want Out!

Even though I was serving in my ideal location, Germany, this was no guarantee I would thrive there. In fact I began experiencing home-sickness and other difficulties adjusting to army life. One year into my Germany assignment, the type of work I was doing became routine, technical, and boring to me. Unconsciously I began looking other places for challenge and excitement.

I found myself driving into Nurnberg some nights and weekends. I longed for more opportunities to use my German and to meet German people. I observed gay men looking for sexual encounters, especially in public restrooms. I also began noticing some men on the streets who would give signals with their eyes. They would often stare at their target, scanning him from head to toe and seeking to make eye contact. It didn't take long for me to start connecting with various gay German men. We would have brief sex together in anonymous encounters. I wanted to keep it that way, so I never gave out my full name, phone number, or address.

I had learned to drink during my college year in Germany, where beer and wine are consumed much as we drink soda pop and coffee. In the Army I started to go out drinking with buddies, or sometimes alone. I found I liked the way alcohol helped me relax and deal with stress. Little did I realize at first how my inhibitions would diminish when I indulged too much. Normally, when I was sober, I would not allow my words or actions to reveal my strong sexual attraction to certain men. But when I drank too much, I would unconsciously let down my guard and say or do something inappropriate. For example, I would stare at a man, or I might even come up from behind and touch him on the buttocks, hoping for a positive response.

Alcohol—beyond a couple of beers—is not good for me. It causes me to forget restraint and to say and do whatever feels good at the time. During my Army years, and beyond, it usually endangered me by opening the door to my same-sex addiction.

My homosexual encounters escalated to the point that I felt out of control. I would enjoy momentary pleasure from sexual activity, yet I knew it was wrong. Guilt would come quickly and I'd ask God to forgive me. But I felt trapped. I wanted to stop, but found it impossible.

As a Christian I believed this behavior was sin and displeasing to God. I enjoyed reading God's Word, praying, and attending church. Yet these things became more difficult for me as my sexual addiction increased. I felt God must hate me for my behavior and lustful thoughts. How could God put up with me? How could He keep forgiving me for repeating the same sins over and over? Why would God not "change" me and remove those desires? I had prayed and begged God many times to change me. It was not happening.

My fear of being found out by Army people was increasing. I felt I could not handle the embarrassment and likely rejection if my peers knew about me. I decided I would try to get out.

Once I decided to try for an early discharge based on my problem, I had to devise how to do it. I was not sure whom to speak with first. I realized I needed to follow the chain of command. But how could I work up the courage to begin telling them of my struggle?

Finally, out of desperation I spoke with the sergeant above me. I requested to talk with the company commander, citing "personal problems." He didn't press for more details, for which I was grateful.

My request went up the line, and I was given approval. William Freeland was a first lieutenant and company commander for the 182nd Light Equipment Maintenance Company in North Bavaria. As I sat in his office for the first time, I was nervous and fearful of how he might respond. I told him about my out-of-control homosexual behavior and shared that this was inconsistent with my Christian beliefs. I needed to get out of the Army in order to receive much-needed help.

I also emphasized to Lieutenant Freeland that I was afraid of what others in the Army would think if they knew this about me. So I asked him to keep it confidential. He agreed with this and shared that he also was a Christian. Then he clarified that this request might take some time to process and would likely need to go up to the brigade level for a decision.

It was easier to talk with Lieutenant Freeland than I had expected. He told me he would pray for me and for God's will to be done. God blessed and encouraged me with this sensitive, compassionate Christian company commander. In order to keep this more confidential, he suggested that I type out the letter for his superior officer, which I did. He allowed me to use his office to type the letter at night.

After waiting a few weeks, I was informed that I would need to meet with an army psychiatrist several times for his assessment and recommendation. He asked me lots of questions, some of which were very embarrassing. Eventually he asked me if I'd ever had sex with a woman and I said no. Then he proceeded to tell me I should start having sex with women, and I would learn to find it pleasurable. He said he believed this was just a passing phase and that I would "outgrow" it. I don't recall him giving any indication that I could be discharged based upon my struggle.

I kept waiting, hoping, and praying. At last, three or four months after my initial request, I got the official response from the brigade headquarters. My company commander told me that my request was denied. He explained that there was not enough evidence of my problem. I would not be granted an early discharge for this unless I was "caught in the act" of having homosexual sex with another Army man. If that happened, I would receive a dishonorable discharge. I surely did not want that, and was very discouraged with the decision. Yet I resolved to make the best of my remaining two years.

The Slow Countdown

I had done more than eight months of volunteer work for the Chaplaincy Department when I learned that one of the chaplain's assistants was returning home. I asked about the possibility of taking his place. I had not been trained for that position, but felt I could do it. I interviewed with the Protestant chaplain, Major Neal J. Harris, for the position. He requested that I be transferred to become one of his two assistants. To my delight, it was approved and I began working with him in the early summer of 1969.

Over the next two years I served as a chaplain's assistant for two different Protestant chaplains: Chaplains Harris and Johnson. I would also help at times with the district chaplain, Lieutenant Colonel William Fosmire. And I helped the Catholic and Jewish chaplains in a variety of ways, such as doing office work in the place of an absent assistant.

All chaplain's assistants were enlisted men who served in a wide variety of capacities. Each of us was like an administrative assistant, doing general secretarial work, receiving and making phone calls, filing, helping with correspondence, running errands and conducting the weekly worship services, among other duties. We were required to be flexible and skilled in interacting with a broad range of people: both enlisted people and officers, as well as civilians—both American and German.

My struggles and homosexual encounters with strangers continued during those last two years, although more sporadically and with decreasing frequency. I was constantly torn between my fleshly desires and my desire to grow in faith and cultivate increasing obedience to God. My self-image was very low. I felt that God must be very displeased with me and did not love me as much anymore due to my continued disobedience.

I very much enjoyed my work as a chaplain's assistant. This helped offset my low self-esteem and gave me some hope. What a delight for me to be daily interacting in that context with such a wide variety of people. My love for people, my enthusiasm for life, my communication skills, my music skills (especially piano and singing), along with my love for God, all seemed to help lessen the frequency of my homosexual behavior. I was thankful to be in a position where I could utilize so many of my interests, skills, and gifts.

When I would experience deep feelings of loneliness, homesickness, and failure as a Christian, I would often find myself more vulnerable to homosexual temptation. Too often I'd give in to the temptation and get sexually involved with a stranger. I was never sexually involved with anyone, man or woman, who was serving in the military.

As was typical for me, I would make every effort to keep my gay behaviors a secret from everyone. It seemed nobody suspected that I was gay. I thought if I told anyone, I would be ridiculed, humiliated, and rejected.

A few times I shared about my struggle with others. I told Steve, who worked with me as a chaplain's assistant. He was a good listener and sought to encourage me. When I stayed in the home of Bud and Shirley Hinkson for a week in London, I shared privately with Bud. They were staff with Campus Crusade for Christ whom I had known for numerous years in my hometown. Bud prayed for me, encouraged me, offered hope, and gave me a large *Amplified Bible*. Bud's love for me in spite of my sinfulness was a significant help. He also referred me to a Christian friend in Germany who was a dentist serving with US Army. I visited the dentist, who also encouraged and prayed for me.

In early months of 1970, Uncle Bob and Aunt Nellie came to Europe and traveled and skied with me for a week in Austria. I told Aunt Nellie about my homosexuality, and she responded with kindness, love, and acceptance. (In 1971, after Aunt Nellie had passed away, Uncle Bob came over and we went skiing together for a whole week outside of Innsbruck again.)

In the summer of 1970, one year before I left the army, my parents and sister, Collette (age fifteen), came and visited me for three weeks. We traveled around parts of Europe in my 1968 VW Beetle. What wonderful memories I have of that time with the three of them. We went through much of Germany, Austria, Belgium, and the Netherlands. Two highlights stand out: attending Mozart's *The Magic Flute* at the Vienna opera (where we also spotted actress Claudette Colbert) and attending the world-renowned, all-day *Passion Play* in Oberammergau, which portrays Jesus' life.

During my last year in the Army, I dated a friendly and cute divorced American lady. She was visiting her brother, who was also in the Army in Germany. She had a young son and daughter whom I liked, and they liked me. She and I went for a short trip to Amsterdam and shared the same bed in a hotel. We became intimately involved, but no intercourse. I had previously told her of my same-sex struggles. We corresponded often after she returned home to the States. I thought we might eventually get married. I surely enjoyed her as a good friend, yet was not interested at that time in having sexual relations with any woman.

I decided I wanted to attend seminary in preparation for ministry. I deliberated between Western Seminary in Portland, Oregon; Dallas Seminary in Dallas, Texas; and Capital Seminary in Worthington, Ohio. I finally settled on Capital Seminary—a Lutheran school—even though I had been raised in a Conservative Baptist church. The Lutheran chaplain I worked for highly recommended it, so I applied and was accepted. *Of course it was a nice coincidence that my girlfriend—and possible future wife—just happened to live in the same city!* My goal was to finish seminary and likely return to Germany or perhaps Austria, where I could use my German language ability as a missionary.

Looking Forward, Looking Back

"Short! Short! I'm a short-timer!" we'd often say as our time drew closer to getting out of the Army. I had strong, mixed feelings about leaving. On one hand, I was thrilled to be getting out of the Army and to begin seminary studies. On the other hand, I was sad to be leaving Germany, which I had come to love deeply.

I wish I had known then what I know now, especially regarding homosexuality and its causes, as well as things that help in the healing process. I wish I'd known then how to combat temptations with God's help and power. Mostly, I wish I had known God then like I know Him now through His Word and through personal experiences. I could have avoided so many, many problems that worsened over the following years.

In addition, I strongly regret the very negative, sinful influence I had on some people due to my sexual behavior. I wish now that I had been steadily growing in my relationship with God, living in obedience and freedom, so I could have more boldly shared God's love and the gospel with others.

Chapter 5

Seminary Years

For his anger lasts only a moment, but his favor lasts a lifetime; weeping may remain for a night, but rejoicing comes in the morning.

—King David, Psalm 30:5, NIV

Through many dangers, toils and snares,
I have already come;

—John Newton, "Amazing Grace"

What am I doing here in a gay bar, drinking, dancing, and "cruising"? I feel so lonely and confused. I hope I can find a good-looking, friendly man here who will also be attracted to me. That man over there surely has a good-looking body. He's a bit taller than me . . . Yes, I wish I were taller than I am. He's got a full head of hair, and I'm sitting here, mostly bald, and feeling self-conscious. He is so very handsome . . . Oh, how I wish I were handsome, then other men might be more attracted to me. He seems to be alone and looking for someone, just as I am. My eyes begin looking him over in more detail, and I begin to wonder and fantasize what it may be like to have sex with him. Finally I work up my courage to go over and ask him for a dance, and to my surprise

*and delight he accepts. We begin dancing casually at
first, then begin to get closer together and more intimate.*

*We stop dancing and have a beer together. As I
drink more beer, I find I lose more and more of my resis-
tance and inhibitions. Eventually he asks me if I'd like
to go somewhere, and I agree. We drive to a secluded
spot and have sex. At first I feel like anything is okay, no
holding back, total freedom and abandonment to sexual
pleasure. Then when we are done satisfying each other,
in creep the same old familiar feelings of shame and guilt.
He asks for my name and phone number, but I give him
a false name and no phone number.*

After being discharged from the Army at Fort Dix, New Jersey, I went to visit Capital Seminary in Ohio, where I met some faculty and even saw the dorm room I would inhabit. I also visited my girlfriend, who was eagerly anticipating my seminary sojourn in her town. I left there and came home to Oregon to see my family and friends, gather up my things, and return to Ohio in a few weeks.

As it so "happened," I visited Western Seminary in Portland to see some college friends. On new student registration day. The registrar, Dr. Donald Launstein, asked me why I was not coming to Western and urged me to reconsider my decision. I agreed to pray about it. I told him that in order to change direction completely, I would have to know for sure that it was God's will, beyond a doubt. I went home (then in Salem) and told my parents that I might change my plans and attend seminary in Portland. I paid a visit to my longtime friend, Larry Dickson, in Eugene. I talked and prayed with Larry and spent time praying alone. And after I wrestled with the decision, God clearly showed me He wanted me to go to Western Seminary. So that's what I did.

It was no easy decision. Among other difficulties, I would be living far from my girlfriend. But that problem was resolved quickly when I came to my senses. I didn't want to marry a divorcee, nor did I want an instant family. I soon called off the relationship.

True Brothers

As I began my studies, I lived in Milliken Hall, the men's dormitory, with all our meals provided in the dining room six days a week—no meals on Sundays. I lived in the dorm for about a year and a half, then moved off campus and shared an apartment, and still later shared a large house.

The seventies look

Living in the men's dorm provided me with a generous number of new friends who loved God and were training to serve Him in ministry. We shared our lives together, eating, studying, praying, playing. I enjoyed playing ping pong with some of the men after dinner, before studying the rest of the night. I enjoyed running with some of them regularly for exercise. I have kept in touch with many of them over these past forty years. How refreshing to be in an environment of love and desire to serve God. I did not miss the cussing and negativity I had found in the Army.

My first few months in seminary were wonderful, though stretching because of the graduate-level studies, and because I'd been out of school for four years. What a blessing to study God's Word daily, more in-depth than ever before in my life. I began soaking up the Bible, my faith was increasing, and I was rejoicing in the challenges and opportunities. I thought I was experiencing a little taste of heaven. I had some sexual temptations, but they were not overwhelming and I resisted them.

Then after about two months I began to experience stronger temptations to give in to my homosexual urges. I was feeling increasingly stressed from studies and loneliness on the weekends. Many of my colleagues were either married or dating on weekends. I was neither married nor dating. One weekend I went driving in downtown Portland and began noticing many men in their twenties and thirties and even some teenagers cruising the streets, looking for other men. I parked my car and before long I was inside a gay bar for what I believe was my first time. I felt awkward and out of place, yet I was drawn like a magnet to stay and see what was happening. Many of the men were openly hugging, touching, kissing, and dancing with each other.

I was soon frequenting gay bars, usually leaving with a man to have sex. I enjoyed the sexual pleasure and, at a deeper level, I felt wanted and valued—an emotional hunger that I longed to satisfy. But soon afterward I would feel dirty and guilty and fearful. I did not tell anyone I met much about myself. I did not give out my address or phone number, as I wished to remain anonymous and only have one-time encounters.

After each sexual encounter, I would pray and ask God for forgiveness. I would ask Him—no, *beg* Him—to take away those wrong desires and to heal me.

God did neither of those things at that time. Looking back now, I realize that I was very confused and felt an overwhelming need to connect strongly with other men. Sex was the main way I knew how to relate at a more intimate level. I would ask God to forgive me and take away the desires and temptations and change me. At the same time I could not begin to imagine how I would survive without such connections with men. I was familiar with the many recorded miracles God had done in the Bible, so I knew He could change me. *If* He *wanted* to. When He did not perform the miracle, I would tell myself that it was because my life was such an ugly mess and I did not deserve any miracles.

I would waiver back and forth and repeatedly promise God that I would never do it again. I could not keep that promise.

Apparently I did a good job of keeping my private life secret. I projected a believable facade. I've asked several of my friends and roommates from this period whether they suspected I was gay, and most have said no.

Finally, three or four months after I began seminary, I desperately felt I must talk with somebody. I could not keep it to myself any longer. But who could I trust? Who might understand, or at least be sympathetic to my intense struggle? One night after supper a number of us went downstairs and played some ping pong, as we often did. Then we went to our respective rooms to study. I worked up the courage to ask Dan Britts, who roomed next door to me, to go to the prayer room to pray together. He agreed.

Out of desperation, as well as my trust in Dan, I was able to tell him what was bothering me. As I began telling him of my deep struggles with homosexuality over numerous years, I noticed his eyes filling with tears. Right away I sensed he cared, he hurt with me, and he wanted to help if he could. I had told various other people of my struggle, but not many. Each time it was very difficult. This time seemed different. He asked me a few questions for clarification, but he did not interrogate me for details.

Dan Britts was a blessing from God at the right place and the right time. He admitted openly that he did not know much about homosexuality and that he had only known a few "gay" men in college. However, Dan assured me that he would seek to learn what he could in order to help me. He did not hesitate to assure me of God's love for me, and also of his own love for me as a brother in Christ. I gradually felt a bit more relaxed and hopeful. Dan said he would make himself available to me anytime day or night to talk or pray together. I sensed in that moment that he really meant it, but I would not know with certainty until I put him to the test over and over again in the coming months and years. Finally I'd discovered a loving, merciful, compassionate, forgiving friend who would share my burden and offer hope and help that I so desperately needed.

Dan promised to keep my struggle a secret between us. In fact he kept his promises to me at every level. He sacrificially and compassionately made himself available to meet with me or take my call, often in the middle of the night when I was overcome with sin and shame and guilt. He was a good listener and knew when to be silent and when to speak. He freely allowed God's love and forgiveness and hope to flow through him to me over and over again. This good man, more than anybody else, taught me the true meaning of friendship.

Dan Britts, 1997

Dan became to me like "God with skin on." It was only a few years ago that I realized what was really happening between Dan and me. It was not Dan alone who related to me so powerfully. Biblically, I believe that God indwells each believer through His Holy Spirit. So as Dan was indwelt by God, God related to me through Dan. When I'd look into Dan's blue eyes and sense his love and compassion, it was *God* looking at me through Dan's eyes! When Dan would hug me, it was really God hugging me. When Dan would speak words of loving encouragement, it was God speaking! This might seem obvious to some readers, but for many years I did not understand it.

Pilgrim's Progress?

So passed my first three years of seminary. I was deeply challenged and stretched mentally, physically, and spiritually. Each of those three areas provided both challenges and blessings.

Mentally, the wide range of courses I took was very enriching to me. The ones I enjoyed the most were hermeneutics, homiletics, Bible survey, theology and church history. I also enjoyed studying the two main Bible languages, Hebrew and Greek, in keeping with my love for languages in general.

Physically, I purposefully challenged myself, with the encouragement of others. Upon leaving the army, I was out of shape. I had been working primarily in an office and got little exercise. So I began and continued running regularly with others.

I experienced various illnesses, probably in part due to inner turmoil over my sinful sexual habits.

Clearly, the spiritual dimension proved to be the source of the most significant challenges and blessings. I experienced the whole gamut of ups and downs, victories and defeats, joys and sorrows. At times I climbed the spiritual mountain tops. Then other times I fell to the depths of failure, despair, and hopelessness.

The greatest challenge I faced was learning how to put my faith into practice—that is, to obey God in all things. I was aware of the reality of spiritual warfare, yet I had likely never before experienced it at such a prolonged and intense level. Some might say I was experiencing Paul's description found in Romans 7. Verse 19 sums it up well: "The good that I will to do, I do not do; but the evil I will not to do, that I practice."

Why is it that I kept growing in my knowledge of God and His Word, yet kept increasing in my sinful disobedience? Most of my life I've heard many Christians, including myself, emphasize the importance of reading and studying God's Word. Yet how very well I realize now that gaining more and more biblical knowledge does not guarantee a person's obedience and genuine spiritual growth. I could have spent twenty years in seminary, yet have remained a disobedient, immature believer, bringing shame to my Lord. I understand now more fully that I must not merely *know* God's Word, but I must also make choices and decisions to follow God and obey Him. James states this idea clearly: "Be doers of the word, and not hearers only, deceiving yourselves" (James 1:22).

In those first three years of seminary, God blessed me continually by enabling me to persevere with my studies in the midst of enormous struggles and fears. God graciously provided me with the experience of making and cultivating friendships with many people among the students, faculty, and staff.

An unseen blessing to me was God's frequent protection of me from the evil one. Even though I repeatedly gave in to temptation, I realize now that Satan could have completely defeated me, yet God intervened on my behalf and to my benefit over and over again. I deeply regret the defeats, but even more I treasure the victories.

Still, the defeats were plenty. And they took their toll. I rationalized my pattern of anonymous, one-time encounters. In some ways I wished I could develop an ongoing relationship with a man, but I realized that would be dangerous. I observed numerous men who had steady lovers, and I envied that security. But if I were to have a steady lover, I felt I'd have to turn my back completely on what I believed about God and His Word.

Over and over I found myself in a gay bar or a bathhouse, looking over all the men, seeking someone attractive who also wanted me. I didn't realize at the time how very selfish and self-centered I was. I so often looked at other men as objects for my own pleasure and satisfaction. I did not think of them as made in God's image and having infinite worth as human beings.

Now I realize that I was obviously a sex addict and that sex was a constant, twenty-four-hour obsession with me. I do not remember consciously making the choice to use sex to medicate my pain. Yet I think that's what I did. The physical and emotional and psychological high from homosexual encounters became increasingly addictive to me.

I learned there was a thriving gay subculture in Portland and I got increasingly involved, yet tried to stay anonymous.

I had never heard of anyone who had successfully overcome homosexual desires and behavior. Yet I kept hoping and praying and seeking secretly for answers and help to change. I recall looking through books and magazine articles about homosexuality in the seminary library; but I was fearful to check them out, for fear someone would suspect my problem.

Looking back at those many years of struggle, I realize I was deceived. I would fluctuate back and forth regarding the seriousness of my homosexual sins. I'd feel like I was the worst of sinners and wondered how God would be able to keep forgiving me, since I could not forgive myself. Then I'd find myself feeling holier than thou, since I was not taking sexual advantage of women. Somehow in my distorted thinking I sensed my homosexual sins were not nearly as serious or gross as some other sins people were committing. Back and forth I'd go in my thinking.

So often I felt like I was an oddity, all alone in my struggle with attraction for the same sex. Other men were seemingly free to talk about and ask for prayer regarding heterosexual lust. But I thought if I was transparent about my feelings and temptations and behavior, they could not handle it and would most likely turn their backs on me.

Flirting with the Precipice

LEND ME YOUR HOPE

Lend me your hope for awhile,
    I seem to have mislaid mine.
Lost and hopeless feelings accompany me daily,
    Pain and confusion are my companions.
I know not where to turn;
    Looking ahead to future times does not bring forth
    Images of renewed hope.
I see troubled times, pain-filled days, and more tragedy.

Lend me your hope for awhile,
    I seem to have mislaid mine.
Hold my hand and hug me;
    Listen to all my ramblings, recovery seems so far distant.
The road to healing seems like a long and lonely one.

Lend me your hope for awhile,
    I seem to have mislaid mine.
Stand by me, offer me your presence, your heart and your love.
Acknowledge my pain, it is so real and ever present.
I am overwhelmed with sad and conflicting thoughts.

Lend me your hope for awhile;
    A time will come when I will heal,
    And I will share my renewal,
    Hope and love with others.

—Author unknown[3]

---

[3] This is an adaptation by Neil T. Anderson of the original anonymous poem, from Anderson's book, *Victory Over the Darkness,* page 20.

I was nearing the end of winter term of my third year. My grades were suffering because of the continual stress of my dual lifestyle. Maintaining a charade of this order takes an amazing toll on one's body and soul. On Friday morning, March 1, 1974, I met with Dr. Crosby Englizian, my church history professor, to discuss options for bringing my grades up. This kind and discerning man could tell that I was struggling with something beyond the academic, and he pressed gently for me to share more. I ended up telling him about my battle with homosexuality. He listened with acceptance, patience, and love—the early stages of a friendship that lasted until Dr. Englizian's death only two years prior to this book's publication.

I walked away from his office feeling a little lighter, assured of his prayers on my behalf. The following was most of my short entry in my journal: "Today I had a very open and honest talk with Dr. Englizian. He said he'd pray about it this weekend." Reading these brief words now, written decades ago, reminds me of the enormous burden of fear and anxiety that I constantly bore, concerned that others would find out about my homosexual thoughts and actions. I was afraid to identify my struggle, referring to it in vague language even in my journal. I also wrote that day that I found especially helpful A.W. Tozer's opening prayer in chapter 9 of *The Knowledge of the Holy*. The final part reads, "We rest in Thee without fear or doubt and face our tomorrows without anxiety."

Saturday was a productive day, solely by God's grace and provision. Then for Sunday, my journal is blank. My guess is that the weight and seriousness of my conversation with Dr. Englizian was beginning to impact me deeply.

On Monday, March 4, I met again with Dr. Englizian, and we agreed that any decision regarding my future at the school needed to include the seminary administration. *More* of the people I admired were going to see my darkest side. My very brief journal entry stated, "I had a very rough time today, especially in the evening when working at the library. I was extremely depressed." Those words were sorely understated, given the thoughts and plans that filled my head that evening.

The Leap

O God, I can't go on. I'm worn out from the struggles for so many years. The battle has been so intense. Worst of all, I have no hope. I can never change . . .

I feel so ashamed. I'm a wretched sinner and cannot change my life. I want to live a pure and holy and righteous life, yet I'm far from that.

I'm filled with fear. If I continue on, people will eventually become aware of who I am and the type of life I've been living. I could not face other people if they knew the many sinful things I've done.

Yes, Lord, I know Your Word says You love me and accept me and have forgiven me of all my sin . . . but I cannot forgive myself, it seems. I feel like You must just "tolerate" me, but You surely cannot love me and be proud of me as Your son.

I have abused Your grace and mercy and forgiveness, and I deserve to die. Why should I go on living, when I am so miserable and have no hope?

Now that I've opened the door to my secrets to my seminary professors, I'll be so embarrassed and humiliated if I continue with my studies.

I believe that if I take my own life, I will go to heaven, because of Your promises in Your Word. Yet I realize I will be at least a bit ashamed and embarrassed to enter heaven by means of taking my own life. What a coward I am. I cannot face my struggle and battle with homosexual temptations and behaviors any longer. I cannot accept or love myself. How can anyone else accept and really love me, especially if they know the real me?

Oh God, where are You? At times in the past, I have sensed Your strong and loving presence. Yet now I feel You have turned Your back on me and left me to suffer alone. I try to talk to You, but You are silent. Truly I feel so all alone, and helpless and hopeless. I guess I cannot blame You for turning away from me. My life is such an ugly mess! You are holy and righteous, so I guess You no longer want to associate with me. I have broken one command after another, and over and over again. I have been unfaithful to

You for so many years. Lord, if indeed You have given up on me, then I will give up on myself also . . .

I don't want to live any more. I must take my life to end this unceasingly hopeless battle and pain.

These and many other thoughts like them flooded my mind in the early days of March 1974, after revealing my struggle to Dr. Englizian. I was gradually distancing myself from others and from life. I was becoming like a zombie. I lacked clear, coherent thoughts.

On Monday night I worked at my part-time job in the seminary library and began making plans to take my life. When I left the library I heard someone singing in the chapel, so I stepped inside and stayed at the back. As much as I love music, this time it did not seem to affect me much. I was resigned to giving up.

I went home late and lay down on my bed. I planned to commit suicide that night by slashing my wrists, so I could "passively" bleed to death. I wanted my roommates to find me the next day, along with the various letters I planned to write. I began thinking of what to include in each of the letters. One to my parents, one to the *Oregonian* newspaper, one to the seminary, one to my roommates, and one to my church.

I wanted to make clear to people the specific reason for my suicide. I did not want there to be any need for guessing or speculating. No! I wanted each to know of my hopelessness and despair. Homosexuality had consumed my life and robbed me of all hope. I thought perhaps some of my readers would take this problem more seriously and seek to help those who want the help. If they did not have the answers, then maybe they would be diligent to find them.

Looking back now, I'm ashamed that I did not give more people a chance to help me. I wish I had had the courage to talk with some of my seminary roommates. They may not have had specific answers, but they could have listened, encouraged me, and prayed. If only I had given them the chance...

It makes me think of John Powell's book, *Why Am I Afraid to Tell You Who I Am?* (Answer: because if I tell you who I am, and you don't like who I am, that's all I have.) I feared rejection, so I stayed in hiding.

Also, it's a mystery to me why I did not talk with Dan Britts about my thoughts of ending my life. He was my best friend, and he had been so very helpful, forgiving, hopeful, and encouraging to me for three years. Yet I did not tell him what I was planning. Most likely because I thought he would try to change my mind, to keep me living and seeking victory over the enemy of my soul. And I didn't think I was up to that. Perhaps I was too ashamed and embarrassed. Or maybe I felt I could handle it on my own and things would get better. Whatever my reasons, it was very unwise for me not to talk with someone as soon as I realized where my thoughts were leading me.

As I lay on my bed that night, thinking through the letters to write, and planning to die in a matter of hours, I was completely exhausted in every way. In fact, it seemed that death would be a most welcome relief.

Without warning, I fell into a deep sleep and did not awaken till the next morning. Was I ever surprised to wake up! *Alive.* I was confused briefly and wondered what had happened and why I was still breathing. Then I realized I'd fallen asleep. Or more accurately, God had put me to sleep. He had also changed my attitude enough that I no longer wished to follow through on my suicide plans.

"I will exult you, O LORD, for you lifted me out of the depths and did not let my enemies gloat over me" (Psalm 30:1, NIV).

Thank You Lord, for not giving up on me, though I gave up on myself! Thank You for gradually renewing my hope and providing me help in so many ways in the coming years. Now I'm grateful to be alive, and I'm grateful for the four decades of life since that night. Thank You, Lord, for the many wonderful experiences and joys with which You have blessed me.

The Circle Widens

I made no entries in my journal for the next four days. I was stressed and confused, seeking to survive in the midst of all the uncertainty surrounding my future, as I would soon likely be withdrawing from seminary. Sometime in these few days I met with Dr. Robert Cook, the seminary vice president, and shared about my struggle. I was in such terrible condition that Dan Britts came with me to this meeting for support. Dr. Cook listened with compassion, expressed many of the same concerns as Dr. Englizian, and decided that I needed to talk to the school president, Dr. Earl Radmacher.

Of all people, Dr. Radmacher was the last I wanted to tell about my sinful lifestyle. I saw him as a powerful and imposing man. Fear was mingled with my appreciation and respect for him. What is more, he had invited me to be his German interpreter on a European teaching tour he had planned for the summer, and I dreaded possibly having to miss out on such a wonderful opportunity.

But in spite of my misgivings I met with Dr. Radmacher that Thursday afternoon and told him the worst about me. Imagine my relief when this man, whom I had respected and feared from a distance, began to shed tears of love and compassionate sorrow. While he empathized with my personal pain, he also took my sin seriously. By this time I knew that leaving the school was a foregone conclusion, and Dr. Radmacher confirmed this. "Jerry," he said, "I feel you need some competent professional counseling. And I think you should withdraw from seminary until your life is under control and you've had time to prove that you're qualified to serve Christ." I would finish out the winter term, and then leave seminary behind.

So it was decided. And yet so much was left suddenly undecided. If I couldn't continue training for ministry, what would I do? And with whom would I do it? I've always needed a circle of support around me, especially in times of crisis. Would the friends I'd made in the last three years continue to be available as I faced the uncertainty ahead?

The good news was that I now desired to keep on living. I was experiencing a gradual renewal of hope. On Thursday evening I wrote a letter to Dr. Radmacher. It started: "As I shared with you briefly this afternoon, this past week had been extremely devastating, even to the point of almost complete despair and hopelessness. Yet that was not the end! God preserved me and lifted me up!" I noted that the Holy Spirit was reminding me of various promises from the Word—especially Isaiah 41:10: "Fear not, for I am with you; be not dismayed, for I am your God. I will strengthen you, yes, I will help you, I will uphold you with My righteous right hand."

My letter continued: "With confidence now I can state that my faith is in God. And although I do not know what the immediate future holds for me, God knows.... He is working to accomplish His ultimate purposes in my life, and will continue to do so until the day of Jesus Christ (Philippians 1:6)." I think this was significant, coming just three days after my plans to end my life.

Small Victories

That Saturday my parents called me, and I told them that my summer ministry with Dr. Radmacher had been postponed. I did not tell them why. I probably also mentioned that I was going to stop my seminary studies for a while and take a break.

In the evening I got in my car and put God aside from my mind, locking Him away in His compartment, preparing to go downtown for a sexual encounter. In that moment the thought came to me—I'm sure it was the Holy Spirit—*Call Dan. Give him a chance. Don't risk your friendship.*

So I stopped at a phone booth and called him. "Dan, I'm calling as you requested and this is before the fact, believe it or not. Please tell me what you want to say and then let me leave."

I can't remember all of his exact words, but his love saturated that phone line: "Jerry, if you hang up that's your business, but I'm not going to hang up. I'm going to stay on the phone until you tell me that you're going back home and going to bed."

"Dan," I said, "how can you do that to me? You know I want to do it. I know what's right, but it's just not that easy. Don't pretend it's so simple."

And so he prayed. I couldn't pray, but he prayed for me. Then he asked for my commitment: "Okay, Jerry, will you go home and go to bed?"

To my surprise, I said, "Yes."

That taught me something very important: I *could* change my behavior, even if it was only for one hour or one day, especially when I cried out for help. Gradually I began to learn that I don't have to go through another mediator to get to God. I can go directly. As I'm going about my day, when a temptation comes to my mind, I can say, "Help me, Lord!" I can't come up with eloquent prayers when I am in the midst of temptation, but I've found that I can fire up two or three words. And if I ask sincerely, God honors my plea every time, almost instantaneously. That's a lesson from which I continue to benefit to this day.

The next evening after my close call I met with Dan at his home, and he counseled with me. He suggested setting up specific goals to assist in overcoming my difficulties.

The next day, exactly one week after wanting to end my life, I wrote in my journal, "Today, I had a very good day of studying, but especially good, as I was able to trust God continually."

In late July, Dan suggested that I make a covenant with God to refrain from any homosexual behavior for six weeks—to the end of August. I made out the covenant, and we both signed it. "What a relief," I wrote, "like a burden lifted! My whole attitude at work was also much better and the work seemed easier."

The next day Mr. Hal Free, a Christian counselor, called to let me know we could begin counseling the next week. This was an answer to months of prayer.

I strongly regret that my seminary studies needed to stop suddenly, just one year away from finishing. At that point I had no idea whether I would return and finish seminary. I wanted to do so, if at all possible.

Chapter 6

Early Marriage Years

When I felt secure, I said, "I will never be shaken."
>—King David, Psalm 30:6, NIV

'Tis grace hath brought me safe thus far,
And grace will lead me home.
>—John Newton, "Amazing Grace"

I first met Rosie Hochstetler (not to be confused with the Rosie I met in college) in early fall 1972, near the beginning of my second seminary year. We were in a large college-career Sunday school class at Hinson Baptist Church in Portland. We became friends, but didn't date for two years. Rosie, along with a few other ladies, would put on a Sunday dinner for some of us seminary students, usually in Rosie's apartment. We would also go on various group outings to places like the zoo or a public park for picnics.

I enjoyed Rosie's friendship and hospitality but had not considered dating her until the end of summer 1974. Rosie was just returning from an eleven-week summer study tour of Israel, sponsored by Western Seminary. I had just recently withdrawn from the seminary.

When I met the returning group at the Portland Airport, something very unexpected and wonderful took place. When I saw Rosie, my eyes were suddenly opened to her beauty and fresh excitement at her summer in Israel. It caught me totally by surprise. *Where has she been all my life?* I wondered. She had lost weight over the summer and was tanned and vivacious. Rosie sparkled like never before, and within a few days I called to invite her on a date.

Rosie, high school graduation, 1967

We discovered that we thoroughly enjoyed being together and sharing life. We would go to movies and eat out, but mostly we enjoyed just talking and hanging out. We could talk about almost anything, and I soon realized Rosie was an excellent listener. I needed someone who cared for me enough to listen and listen well. God provided Rosie.

After we had dated four or five months, our relationship was deepening and possibly headed toward marriage. I wanted to be open with her about my struggle with homosexuality, but I was afraid. She might change her mind and not feel comfortable dating me, or even being my friend. Yet I knew I must take the risk.

One evening at the end of our date we were sitting and talking in my '68 VW Bug. I decided it was time to tell her. I did not share specifics details, but revealed that I had been struggling with homosexuality for many years. I asked what she thought of me now that she knew this. She thought awhile then said she did not think less, but rather more highly of me for having enough courage and love to be honest. I shared that I was doing much better and had been celibate for several months.

We would talk a little about this over the coming months, but never in detail. Rosie might ask how my counseling was going. I would assure her it was going well and that I was staying celibate. I'm thankful that Rosie never pressed me for details, as it would have been very hard for both of us.

Twenty-Five Reasons Why

As I often tell people, the Lord told me in college to marry Rosie; He just didn't give me a last name!

My disastrous marriage proposal to the first Rosie was now history. And the new (and far better, for me) Rosie was becoming my best friend. I decided I would like to marry her and share our lives together. I so enjoyed talking about God and His Word with her. We would often pray together, which helped strengthen our relationship.

Most of my life I had wanted to get married and just assumed that would eventually happen. I looked forward to strong companionship and mutually satisfying sexual intimacy. In addition I had always wanted to have children. My dream was to have identical twins!

I'm mystified how I could believe that everything would turn out fine once I was married, even though my sexual attraction was for men. Somehow I simply assumed that my sexual desires would change once I was married to a woman whom I loved.

I decided to propose on Mothers' Day, May 11, 1975. Being the romantic I am, I wrote a list of twenty-five reasons why I loved her. That special Sunday afternoon I drove Rosie to the top of Mount Tabor, facing west across Portland. We sat and talked as we took in the beautiful panorama. Then I took out my list to read to her. When I finished I asked if she would marry me. She paused and then said *yes*. Over the years, Rosie has often told people that she "prayed and fasted for thirty seconds and said yes."

We met with our pastor, Don Baker, to ask his advice about getting married. He told us he thought it was wonderful. Then he suggested since we were both mature in age and strong Christians that we have a short engagement to reduce the chances of becoming sexually intimate prior to marriage. We met with him several times to plan the specifics of our large wedding, but didn't reveal my struggle with homosexuality. We did not receive premarital counseling. I wish we had, as it may have caused us either to delay our marriage, or at least to be better prepared for it.

Two months after becoming engaged we married at Hinson Memorial Baptist Church in Portland. What a beautiful, sunny, summer day it was! July 19, 1975, was a major milestone in our lives. We were both convinced that God had brought us together, and we were grateful.

My brother, George, was my best man, and my other groomsmen were Rosie's brothers (Stan and Dale) and Dan Britts. Rosie's four bridesmaids were Dorothy, Nancy, "Gigi" (Rosie's sister), and Collette (my sister). We had carefully chosen music for the service, including "Jesu, Joy of Man's Desiring" as the processional, "Savior, Like a Shepherd Lead Us" as a duet, and "The Wedding Prayer," which I sang as a surprise to our guests. It was not listed in the program, in case I was too nervous to sing it. Beethoven's "Ode to Joy" was the recessional.

What a wonderful wedding ceremony and reception we shared, along with over four hundred guests. Finally we took off in my tan VW Beetle.

We honeymooned on the Oregon Coast for almost a week, first in Lincoln City, then at the Alpine Chalets near Otter Rock, and finally one night in Florence.

My naiveté about the physical aspects of women made the honeymoon a bit of a challenge for me, but also an opportunity to learn. By God's grace, we enjoyed wonderful sexual intimacy that first night together. And the sexual enjoyment continued throughout our honeymoon and through the early months of our marriage.

The Snake in the Garden

As the weeks passed, I began comparing my sexual intimacy with Rosie and the sexual fantasies and experiences I had had over the years with men. On the one hand, I knew what aroused men and what brought them the most satisfaction. Yet on the other hand, I was very poorly informed about what aroused women and brought them the most satisfaction.

I realized I was in over my head. For years I had been seeking men to meet my sexual desires and needs. And I had been very selfish in my quest. Now, in marriage, my primary focus shifted. I wanted to grow deeply in my love for Rosie and in my ability to bring her sexual satisfaction and overall fulfillment in our relationship.

I know that everyone faces adjustments at the outset of marriage, but even more so when one of the spouses has been consumed with same-sex desires and experiences. I felt increasingly like a failure in most areas of my life in those early years. I thought I was failing as a husband, provider, lover, and Christian.

I feared others discovering my same-sex attraction, so I made Rosie promise she would tell no one. Rosie honored this request. Looking back, that was selfish, unkind, and unwise of me.

After three months of marriage I began a vicious cycle that became three years of unfaithfulness to Rosie. I sporadically sought out sex with other men in public places. After each sinful encounter I would confess to Rosie and seek her forgiveness. To my surprise, Rosie would forgive me right away. She could tell I was a tormented man, fighting this sexual addiction and seeking victory over it. We would pray together and pour our hearts out to God, for His help, for renewed hope, and for complete victory over my struggle. (Each time I felt that that would be my last time to fail.)

After about a year of my infidelity to her I asked her forgiveness once again, and she quickly forgave me. Puzzled, I asked her how she could keep on forgiving me over and over. Rosie replied, "I was twenty when I became a Christian. God has forgiven me of everything, so who am I not to forgive you?"

O joy beyond description,
O joy beyond degree,
O joy in knowing Rosie
Will always be with me.

O love beyond description,
O love beyond degree,
O love that comes from Rosie
And freely given me.

O peace beyond description,
O peace beyond degree,
O peace that comes from knowing
We're both at peace with Thee!

—Jerry W. Heacock (February 29, 1976, seven months into our marriage, one morning after I had been unfaithful and Rosie had forgiven me)

Rosie's family: Dale, Marion, us, Irene, Stan

My family: George, Collette, us, Mom, Dad

The new "Mrs. Wonderful"

"Mr. Wonderful" and George

It has been in these situations that Rosie's listening gift has been such a marvelous gift to me. My words aren't adequate to describe the value of Rosie's listening ear, so I'll borrow some words from the Roman philosopher and statesman Seneca:

> For who listens to us in all the world, whether he be friend or teacher, brother or father or mother, sister or neighbor, son or ruler or servant? Does he listen, our advocate, or our husbands or wives, those who are dearest to us?
>
> Do the stars listen, when we turn despairingly away from man, or the great winds, or the seas or the mountains? To whom can any man say—Here I am! Behold me in my nakedness, my wounds, my secret grief, my despair, my betrayal, my pain, my tongue which cannot express my sorrow, my terror, my abandonment.
>
> Listen to me for a day—an hour!—a moment! Lest I expire in my terrible wilderness, my lonely silence! O God, is there no one to listen? Is there no one to listen? You ask. Ah yes, there is one who listens, who will always listen. Hasten to him, my friend! He waits on the hill for you. For you, alone.

Me? A Salesman?

Shortly after I left Western Seminary, I worked six months loading and unloading large freight trucks—hard physical labor for my small build. It was quite a relief when, in the early part of 1975, I began working full-time for Aetna Life Insurance Company in Portland. I liked continually meeting new people and being my own boss—scheduling my own appointments, competing with other salespeople for awards, and the like. And I had some good times with my fellow workers. But I found it difficult to make a living from insurance sales. My commission-based income was unpredictable month to month. It was often feast or famine. Mostly famine. I had trouble disciplining my time. Also, major turmoil in other aspects of my life made it difficult to succeed in sales.

After several years with Aetna I left to work for New York Life. I did poorly and lasted less than a year. Then I tried Prudential Life Insurance, where everyone was crowded into one open office, but I could not work well with the constant distractions. So I went back to Aetna and a seventeenth-floor office with a spectacular view of Mt. Hood, East Portland, and the Willamette River. I thought I had arrived. But still struggled with sales, so I got out of insurance sales for a while.

Throughout these years of inadequate income my feelings of failure increased. My struggles with homosexuality were intense in those first three years of marriage. Perhaps I sought to find the success I lacked in sales by having sex with men. If other men desired me sexually, then I must not be totally worthless. My relationship with Rosie was often difficult, and I believed it was mostly my fault. I did not know how to be the husband she wanted and deserved.

Children? Children!

Rosie and I began talking children soon after our engagement. One of us—probably me, since I'm the more talkative—said, "All my life, I've wanted to grow up, get married, and have children. In fact, I've especially wanted to have identical twins." And to our mutual surprise and delight the other responded, "All my life, *I've* wanted to get married, have children, and especially identical twins!" You see, my mom has an identical twin sister, and I had witnessed the special closeness between them. I'd often wished I'd had a twin brother.

Rosie and I agreed to wait awhile before having children. We both had full-time jobs and were struggling financially. One and a half years into our marriage we decided to start trying, but it took longer than expected for Rosie to get pregnant. We both went in for testing, and both were found normal.

Finally, in September 1977 Rosie became pregnant! She did not tell me right away, but waited until she was sure. She broke the news to me on December 6. She treated me to dinner at Sweet Tibbie Dunbars—the first time we'd ever eaten there. After we had ordered our meal, Rosie handed me a note in a small envelope. I opened it and read:

What a surprise and joy! I didn't notice until she pointed out to me later that the small envelope in which she placed the note was in the shape of a diaper.

```
December 6,1977

Sweet Ach:

Rejoice with me in the news of
our first child on July 30,1978.

Let us lift our hearts and praise
God together for the child He will
bring into our lives.

Congraduations Daddy!

All my love,

           Rosie
```

When it finally dawned upon me what was going on, I jumped up and down a few times and shouted. The waitress came over and asked if everything was okay, and I said, *"Oh yes—we're pregnant!"*

I paid no attention to what I was eating. We agreed to tell both sets of parents right away. So we went to a flower shop after dinner and bought numerous pink and blue carnations. We first stopped and told Rosie's parents and gave them some of the flowers. Then we hopped on the freeway and hurried south to Salem. We told my parents the wonderful news also and gave them flowers. Rosie and I *floated* back to Portland, joyous beyond words.

Ever since we'd begun trying to get pregnant, we'd been praying specifically for identical twins. But, we chided each other, we did not want to be too choosy, so we'd leave it to Him to decide whether they would be twin boys or twin girls.

We began thinking of possible names. If we had twin girls, Rosie would choose their names—tentatively Heidi and Heather. And if twin boys, I would select the names—David and Jonathan. What fun! What joy! What expectations and anticipation we shared!

Just a few days before Christmas, Rosie miscarried. I rushed her to the hospital, but it was too late. What a huge loss. What unspeakable sadness. The doctor did not tell us, and we did not think to ask, whether we had lost a single child or twins.

As I recall, nobody spoke to us in terms of "losing a child" or "death of children." Instead, people said things like "I'm sorry, but don't give up. Try again." We chose to wait a while, as we needed time to recover. Our jobs kept us fully occupied. Over the following months we became aunt and uncle to nieces and a nephew, born to Rosie's two brothers and their wives. We enjoyed the vicarious experience.

Over the next few years we finally decided not to have our own children. A year or so later, Rosie was required to undergo a hysterectomy, permanently ending her childbearing potential. We thought of adopting but never seriously pursued it.

Rosie looks back now and says she got to exercise her mothering instincts helping care for our nieces and nephew. It was not until almost twenty years later that I would strongly sense the need to process and grieve this deep loss.

Two in the Battle

Obedience Versus Disobedience to God

A major lesson God is striving to teach me is this:

> *My obedience to God*
> *Brings glory to Him;*
> *My disobedience to God*
> *Brings dishonor to Him.*

> *When I give in to temptations,*
> *And openly disobey God,*
> *I am asserting myself as master,*
> *And turning away from God.*

> *Disobedience brings discontent,*
> *Unhappiness and frustration;*
> *Obedience brings joy,*
> *Peace and love.*

—Found in a three-ring binder, written by me on April 22, 1978

About two years into our marriage, we went to talk with our pastor, Don Baker, about my struggle with homosexuality. Although he had known me for many years, he was surprised. He referred me to Joel MacDonald, the pastor of discipleship and evangelism, whom I had known as a fellow seminary student. Joel was a big help to me on a weekly basis. Yet, although I was improving some, I could not consistently stop the same-sex behavior.

My self-image as a husband was so very poor in those early years. I was constantly frustrated and disappointed with myself, and fearful, as well as feeling hopeless and helpless. I did not like myself, and I strongly doubted that God, who knew everything about me, could possibly like me, let alone love me. How could He? I was so very unlovely, repeatedly and seriously making light of God's grace and of Jesus' death on the cross. I thought that perhaps He just tolerated me, since He'd obligated Himself to do so in His written Word.

Rosie's responses to me in those early years were supernatural gifts from God—her love, her forgiveness, her mercy, her grace, her patience, her hope, her perseverance . . . Rosie truly became and continues to be a rose that produces a welcoming, delightful, and lasting fragrance to me and to all whose lives she touches. She exemplifies what the apostle Paul spoke of in 2 Corinthians 2:14-16, the "fragrance" of the knowledge of Christ and "the aroma of life leading to life." I began to increase in hope and belief that if Rosie could love me and forgive me, then surely God could also. Through His demonstration of love through Rosie, I gradually came to believe the truth of such Bible passages as Romans 5:8 and 2 Corinthians 5:17,21. I know of no other woman who would have been willing to stay with me, love me, forgive me, and pray for me and with me, as Rosie did.

We established some lifelong friendships in those early years. We especially enjoyed interacting with many young married couples in our Sunday school class at Hinson Church. Now I only wish we had been willing to be transparent with them, or at least some, about our intense struggle. *Right before their unsuspecting eyes, it was seeking to tear us apart and devour us.* How I wish I'd had the courage to humble myself and speak the truth to some fellow believers. Then they might have been willing to join hands with us in the battle against the enemy of our souls—the one who seeks to deceive, destroy, and kill. Rosie and

I desperately needed brothers and sisters to fight alongside us during those years of constant and intense battle.

The Philippian Effect

> Do not be conformed to this world, but be transformed by the renewing of your mind, that you may prove what is that good and acceptable and perfect will of God. (Romans 12:2)

> Whatever things are true . . . noble . . . just . . . pure . . . lovely . . . of good report, if there is any virtue and if there is anything praiseworthy—meditate on these things. (Philippians 4:8)

> I can do all things through Christ who strengthens me. (Philippians 4:13)

Many times I wished in those early years of marriage that we could find the solution to my problem. I realize now that I was assuming the answer would be something that would focus on the outside, stopping my outward, sinful behaviors. I did not understand that God wanted to transform me completely—both *inside* and *outside.* In fact, even as I found God's "solution" for me, I didn't know that He was in the process of healing and restoring me *from the inside out!* And that He would change more than my behaviors—He would begin cleansing even my thoughts, desires, and unconscious dreams.

In fall 1978 Al Wilson was the Sunday school teacher in our young married couples class. He was going to start teaching through the small book of Philippians, and he challenged us to consider memorizing the entire book of Philippians. He promised a copy of the newly released *New International Version* Bible to each person who could recite it from memory.

From childhood I had memorized various verses in the Bible—even one whole chapter, 1 Corinthians 13, toward achieving my God and Country award with the Boy Scouts. Occasionally I found it helpful to refer back to these passages, to bring them up from memory without having to open a Bible. Never had I memorized a whole book of the Bible. That seemed to me like a nearly impossible task. Certainly a whole lot of work! But the more I thought about it, the more I became convinced that I wanted to do it, and that I *could* do it.

Rosie decided not to try it herself, but offered to help me. I appreciated her help; I surely knew I would need it.

At this time Rosie and I were both working at jobs with which we were struggling. Rosie liked her job responsibilities but had a difficult supervisor; going to work for her was a daily obstacle to overcome. As for me—the consummate people person, who enjoys and thrives on being with others—I was working alone at a one-man warehouse operation, shipping, receiving, and stocking freight items. My work felt unbearably monotonous and painful.

Since Rosie and I worked only a couple of miles from each other, we carpooled almost daily, giving us more time together before and after work. I would drive and Rosie would check me on my memory work. She had typed out the entire book (from the *New American Standard Bible*) on three-by-five cards, which were easy to carry around and refer to during the day. I still have those lovingly typed index cards.

At first I began memorizing the words and verses in a rote manner. My only goal was to learn and remember the words in order to complete this challenge and receive a new Bible, and enjoy the satisfaction of a goal completed.

But gradually I began reflecting upon the meaning and significance of the words. My thought life began filling more and more throughout the day with positive, wholesome, truthful thoughts. I began making mental connections between various parts of Scripture, getting the bigger message. I found that, step by step, my faith was increasing and my hope was being renewed day by day. My understanding of God's love for the world—*for me*—was increasing. Then I saw this understanding begin to move from my head to my heart!

It was a long, up-and-down process—a battle at times. *I need to work on my verses today,* I would tell myself. *No, I really don't want to. I would rather think my own thoughts and imagine my own lustful desires being fulfilled.* Some days I would struggle back and forth for just a short while, then resume absorbing God's Word. But other days I would abandon my work on Philippians and let my thoughts wander where they may. Once I let down my guard, I could fool myself into believing I could let my thoughts roam. But this was dangerous and untrue. My thoughts needed to be surrendered to God's will if I was sincere about wanting to love and obey Him.

What an eye opener this was for me. You see, for years I had made a false distinction between one's thoughts and one's behavior. It was okay to think what one wanted; it was only wrong to act upon one's sinful desires. More specifically, I could harbor lustful thoughts and fantasies about men, and that was "okay," or at least not nearly as bad.

Yet, day by day, week by week, I continued memorizing Philippians.

> *What's happening, God?* I remember thinking. *I don't understand what is going on, or why. I don't know how to explain this. I am finding that my desire to obey You and to honor You with my life is replacing my desire to think whatever I want. Lord, could it be that You are changing me from the inside out?*
>
> *Yes, and that this is what You have wanted all along, if only I were willing to let You . . . Oh, Father, for so much of my life I have wanted to honor You and please You with my whole heart. Yet it seemed impossible for me. Now I am finding that as I focus on You day and night, memorizing and meditating on Your Word, You are doing the impossible in my life: You are gaining the victory moment by moment in my thought life.*
>
> *Father, thank You for not giving up on me over these many wayward years of lustful, sex-filled obsessive thoughts and actions. You have demonstrated to me Your longsuffering, Your mercy, Your grace, Your patience, Your unconditional love, and more in so many creative ways.*

What a joy it was for me to share with Rosie what God was doing inside of me.

During the three months it took me to memorize Philippians, Scripture was running through my mind day and night. It was as if my mind was being bathed, cleansed, instructed, and guided by the very words of God!

I began walking in consistent obedience to God in inward and outward sexual purity. Since then the enemy has brought many temptations, and indeed I gave in to one of them about three years later in a relatively tame sexual encounter with a man. Afterward, in deep embarrassment, I confessed to Rosie, to Pastor Baker, and to a team of ministry leaders. All conveyed forgiveness and, while acknowledging the seriousness of the sin, accepted me with unconditional love. Other than that stumble, I've lived since then in outward purity, and I've grown toward an ever-purer thought life.

The life-changing power of God's Word shouldn't surprise me. According to Dr. Haddon Robinson, "The Bible is like the ocean. You can wade in it, feed from it, live on it—or drown in it. But those who take the time to learn its truths and practice them will be changed forever."

Charlie Riggs uses the Navigators' illustration of a hand with a firm grasp on the Bible. The four fingers are labeled *hearing, reading, studying,* and *memorizing,* and the thumb is labeled *meditating.* Riggs says,

> We forget 90 percent of what we hear. If we want to retain knowledge of the Bible, therefore, we must do more than just listen. Scripture memory pays the greatest dividends in Bible knowledge (100 percent), but meditation is necessary to make the Bible a part of one's life. Meditation, giving attention to truth with the intention of doing something about it, is the key to application and assimilation of the Scriptures.[4]

New Life

Along with purity in act and thought came an increasingly positive outlook on my life, a greater acceptance of myself. I became so optimistic that at the start of 1979 I wrote a long and complicated list of goals. For example, I committed to "make every effort to grow in my love for Rosie, so she may become 100-percent convinced in her own

---

[4] Charlie Riggs, *Learning To Walk With God,* 94.

mind that I am the best husband, in all areas, she could ever have." As a goal, I now realize that that wasn't very effective, because it isn't measurable. But it provides a glimpse into my heart's desire at that time.

I also set out to memorize five hundred new verses that year. I made some progress, for which I'm grateful, but nothing near my unrealistic goal.

Another glimpse into this season of healing and growth for me comes from an overnight getaway I enjoyed during February 1980. As I wrote out my prayer, I reflected on some of the victories and defeats in my life over that preceding year. I thanked God for the spiritual lessons He was teaching me and the obedience He was making possible for me. In that year we had experienced many changes and challenges, including job changes and waiting periods between jobs. I would fluctuate between worrying and trusting God. I wrote, "Thank You, Father, for giving me Rosie as my loving wife, who continued to encourage me this past year through some of the difficult times. I am so thankful to You and to her for the faith and trust she continually demonstrated in You as we encountered various problems."

This personal solitude time with God came just three months before we would arrive at one of our life's key turning points. Looking back I believe God was preparing me.

Part II
My Second Thirty-Five Years

INTERLUDE

Just As I Am (1980)

*W*hy is my heart beating so fast? What is going to happen today, once I share? My mind and heart race ahead with all sorts of thoughts and feelings.

This is the day and the chance I have wanted for a long time. I will finally have the opportunity to let others know of my longtime struggle with sin. What will people think? Will they receive what I say with love and compassion and forgiveness? Or will they be so shocked they may not know what to think or say or do? I hope they will be challenged and encouraged by what I say.

Is this really the right thing? Is this the best place, the best time? Oh, Lord, help me. Lord, calm my heart and help me trust You completely for strength to share. And help me trust You totally with whatever happens as a result of my testimony.

Lord, I pray that my words will help some people, who struggle as I did, to have new courage and hope for the future. People need to know it is possible to change. It is possible to learn to live in obedience to God and find victory over any sin, day by day.

I have often thought I would rather die than have my sexual sin become widely known. Now I am facing my greatest fear head on. Yet ironically my greatest fear has become closely intertwined with my greatest desire—to offer practical help and powerful hope to others who struggle with this same type of sin.

I finally have reached the point in my life where I am thinking more about the needs of others than my own. I feel more compelled to speak out when I empathize with the paralyzing fear of others like me. How I wish that I could long ago have heard the testimony of someone who had suffered as I have, who had discovered how to live daily in victory!

Now I will be that *someone* for others.

Just as I am, Thou wilt receive,
Wilt welcome, pardon, cleanse, relieve;
Because Thy promise I believe,
O Lamb of God, I come! I come![5]

---

[5] Charlotte Elliott, "Just As I Am, Without One Plea."

Chapter 7

Standing Naked

O Lord, when you favored me, you made my mountain stand firm; but when you hid your face, I was dismayed.

—King David, Psalm 30:7, NIV

The Lord has promised good to me,
His Word my hope secures;

—John Newton, "Amazing Grace"

I had been learning to walk day by day in victory over addiction to homosexuality since the fall of 1978. For most of two years I had been tasting the joy of obedience. God had broken my chains of enslavement to homosexual lusting and behaviors. I increasingly wanted to share my story publicly, and had been asked to do so by both Pastor Baker and Dr. Radmacher. But Rosie had not been ready.

Then as Mother's Day 1980 approached, I felt I could no longer keep my story to myself. I had to share it. I sensed it was much needed and might provide some help and hope to others who were struggling with this same area of sin. I once again asked Rosie if she was ready for me to share my story publicly. This time she said yes! She was neither hesitant nor fearful, but shared my hope that it might help others.

I called Pastor Baker and asked permission to share my testimony in Hinson Church's worship services. He was preparing a sermon on the topic of prayer for Mother's Day and said that my testimony would be very appropriate and powerful as an illustration about the power of prayer.

Rosie and I met with him on Saturday morning, the day before I shared. He did not know whether the church family would be able to handle my story. Nobody had ever shared something like this before at Hinson, so it would be a huge test. Pastor Baker couldn't say for sure, but he hoped the church body would respond with love and forgiveness, proving to be a redemptive, forgiving body. He said that regardless of the church family's response, once I shared my story publicly, I would feel freer than ever before. I would no longer need to live in constant fear of others finding out about my deep, dark secret. And he was right!

On Sunday morning during my devotional time I read Psalm 30 in the NIV and noted, as I often had before, the parallels between my life and King David's words in the psalm. My weeping had lasted through my long night of sin, but now was my morning of rejoicing (verse 5). God had "turned my wailing into dancing" (verse 11). I wrote in my journal, "Today . . . I have the immense joy and responsibility of sharing the love, patience, and forgiveness of God, and the completeness of God's adequacy in giving me victory and freedom from enslavement to this sinful lifestyle. For the first time in my life, I AM FREE!"

The Telling

On Sunday, May 11, 1980, at Hinson Church, I publicly shared my testimony for the first time. What a big risk as I stood "naked" before the congregation, sharing my soul and the darkest secret of my sinful life. As I shared, God reminded me that He had accepted me with all my sin, brokenness, guilt, and shame. He saw my nakedness and clothed me with His robe of righteousness. Praise God! I had received the much-needed gifts of forgiveness and renewed hope, for which I will be eternally grateful.

I spoke in all three morning worship services, one of which was broadcast over KPDQ-FM radio to an estimated listening audience of 50,000 people. We had invited my parents to attend, and my mom was with us in all three services, but my dad was in Alaska on business. We had invited Rosie's family to attend, but instead they listened to the service on the radio. Looking back, I wish all of our parents and many other relatives and friends could have been there in person that day.

When I faced the greatest fear in my life on that Sunday morning, I was not alone. I am convinced now, more than ever, that I would not have been able to do that alone. I was terrified, and I had only gotten three hours of sleep the night before. Truly, the Lord picked me up, held me close, and carried me through that whole morning. My favorite poem, "Footprints" by Margaret Fishback Powers, helps paint a picture of what took place. The poem is about a dream in which the writer sees her life represented by footprints on a sandy beach. For most of her life she sees two sets of footprints side by side, "one belonging to me and one to my Lord." But during the most difficult parts of her life she sees only one set of footprints and, bewildered and accusing, she says,

> "I just don't understand why, when I needed You most,
> You leave me."
> He whispered, "My precious child,
> I love you and will never leave you
> never, ever, during your trials and testings.
> When you saw only one set of footprints
> it was then that I carried you."[6]

Near the end of his sermon on prayer Pastor Baker called me up to join him at the pulpit. He put his arm around me and told the congregation that I had something to share with the church.

"My name is Jerry Heacock," I began, "and I've been a member of this church for the last eight years. I was a student at Western Seminary for three years, a former Sunday school teacher, a class officer, and a committee member of this church.

"The most important decision of my life I made when I was in the first grade, and that was to ask Jesus Christ to come into my life. *And He did!*"

The moment of revelation was almost here. The congregation watched silently, expectantly. I swallowed and continued.

"About three years ago I began getting counseling from Pastor Baker and later from Joel MacDonald. I told them both I wanted to be freed from my—" My heart raced a little faster. "—my homosexuality." There.

---

6   From Margaret Fishback Powers, *Footprints: The Story Behind the Poem that Inspired Millions,* Toronto: Harper Collins, 1983, 9.

It was out. "And since then God has led me into a freedom from this practice. I asked the pastor if I could share briefly with you, and he agreed."

At that point Pastor Baker and I switched to a question-and-answer presentation, he asking and I answering from notes I had written out in preparation. We briefly surveyed my history of same-sex attraction and behavior, from childhood up to recent years, along with my corresponding decline in self-image and consideration of suicide. I told how I had longed to be free of the temptation and sinful lifestyle.

I strongly affirmed God's faithfulness to me through those years. And I spoke glowingly of Rosie's unflinching forgiveness and love in the face of my repeated unfaithfulness.

"Do you believe God made you a homosexual?" Pastor Baker asked at one point.

"No," I answered. "I believe God made me in His image and likeness, as the Bible says, and God is without sin. Therefore, it would be a complete contradiction for God to cause me to practice a sin that He hates."

As much as God hated my sin, I also affirmed that He has always loved me. "I know now that God has forgiven all my sins, so I am at peace with Him and free from guilt."

In connection with the sermon's theme of prayer, I explained, "Unless God had provided His power for me in response to the prayers of myself and others, it would have been impossible for me to gain freedom from homosexual behaviors and thoughts. God's Word clearly tells us of His unlimited power in response to prayer. In Philippians 4:6-7 we are told, 'Be anxious for nothing, but in everything by prayer and supplication, with thanksgiving, let your requests be made known to God; and the peace of God, which surpasses all understanding, will guard your hearts and minds through Christ Jesus.'"

As an example of answered prayer, I told about my friend Dan Britts and his amazing loyalty. Specifically, I told about the night I called him from the phone booth, on my way downtown, and how Dan's earnest prayers for me changed my mind that night. "Praise God," I added, "for His undying love and patience with me."

Then I turned to the watching congregation. "For the past twenty-five years I have fought the battle to keep my homosexuality a secret; today I am voluntarily coming 'out of the closet' and telling you publicly of my major problem in life. Praise God, He heard and answered many specific prayers for me from His people, who knew of my need. Come and rejoice with me. *I am free!*

"I can honestly say I have no desire to return to the homosexual lifestyle. However, as a human being, easily capable of sinning again and again, I know I could give in again at some time to my sinful, physical desires. Therefore, I am sharing myself with all of you, as my church family, and asking you—no, I am *begging* you—for your prayer support on my behalf, that I might continue fervently in my obedience to God.

"I firmly believe this body is capable of forgiving and accepting me. Not in your own human strength, but in the fullness of God's resources you are able to forgive and love."

I lowered my notes and—apprehensive, uncertain, relieved—I glanced at Pastor Baker. He smiled at me, then spoke directly to the congregation. "You have listened to Jerry's story and his request for your forgiveness and acceptance. What is your response? Will you forgive and accept him?"

Silence.

Then, "Yes," said a voice from the crowd. Then another. And another. This led to a few claps, which crescendoed to a roar of applause, complemented by nodding heads and encouraging smiles.

I was overwhelmed by the church family's grace and love for me. After each of the three services, many people came up to my wife and me to express their love and forgiveness, and to hug us. The second and third services were delayed due to the swarm of people waiting to see us. It was not easy to share my story three services in a row, but after the first service I shared with greater courage, already having seen how people responded with so much love.

Letters

Monday morning, May 12

Dear Jerry and Rosie:

As I sit to write I see evidences of your love all around me. . . . All these remind me daily [that you are] very precious to my heart. I thought of [you] dear ones all day yesterday, last night, and this morning. I have wept many tears as I try to imagine your pain of years past—and present. I have prayed almost incessantly—in thanksgiving for your valiant courage and devoted love—and in intercession for your encouragement in the days ahead.

I could hardly teach yesterday simply because my heart was reaching out to you, as I knew you were upstairs revealing yourself again and again. . . .

Please don't let the arch deceiver make you think you are worse than others. That is a lie. God loves you, I love you, the church loves you—the class loves you. I wish you could have experienced their deep love for you yesterday—and the pain each member felt for you, knowing the pain you were experiencing.

Yesterday you stood tall. It took great courage and great love to become vulnerable. I have been praying for this kind of openness between Christians and for our class, so that we could bear one another's burdens. I think you have opened a door for us that no one else has had the courage to open. Through that opening there is flooding light and love.

God bless you. I love you both very much.

Al [Wilson, young marrieds Sunday school teacher, died early November 2014]

Philippians 1:6

When I read this letter for the first time, I was deeply moved and encouraged by Al's kind and loving words. As I rediscovered this letter in preparation for this book, I have read it over numerous times and have been blessed again each time.

Just eleven days after sharing my testimony at Hinson I wrote a heartfelt letter to Dan Britts:

May 22, 1980

Dear Dan,

> The Lord's loving kindnesses indeed never cease,
> For His compassions never fail.
> They are new every morning;
> Great is Thy faithfulness.
> Lamentations 3:22-23, NASB

These two verses came to my mind as I began to collect my thoughts in order to write to you just now. . . . How encouraging these verses were to me as I was in the midst of my inner spiritual struggle for my three years in seminary. These two verses have become even more valuable and encouraging to me over the last few years of our marriage.

Thank you, Dan, for challenging me, and for helping me, and for holding me accountable to memorizing these and other key verses also. What peace and joy the promises in these verses have continually brought me. How wonderful to *know*, and not just hope or wish, that God's loving kindnesses and compassions never cease nor fail. They are new, and unique, and relevant every morning. God's *faithfulness* knows no human comparison, for it is unique, unlimited, eternal, and perfect!

Dan, I wanted to mention, before I forget now, that it is okay with me if you want to share with Sue the main area of struggle in my life . . . . Now that my testimony and major sin problem is "public information," I'm not afraid for people to know this. On the contrary, it gives me unlimited opportunities to praise God and share with others that God wants to, can, and will give us victory in any area.

The exciting thing for me now is that I no longer see myself and my main struggle as hopeless. Instead

I'm gaining a fuller understanding of that victory daily as I completely rely upon the unlimited resources of God. I know if I start getting *over-confident* or self-reliant, then I'm making myself dangerously vulnerable again to attacks from the enemy.

Praise and thanks be to God that He is able to win every battle in my life.

With much love,
Jerry

About two weeks later, Dan wrote in response:

Dear Jerry,

It was neat talking with you on the phone recently and then receiving your letter and tape [of my May 11 testimony]. I am rejoicing with you in the things God is doing in your life.

While listening to the tape, I had a hard time fighting back the tears of joy as I listened to you share. I am very proud of you, Jerry, and appreciated so much the courage, sensitivity, clarity, and joy with which you shared with the congregation. As you suggested, I shared with Sue the struggle which you have had, and she rejoiced with me as she listened to your tape. The response of the congregation to Pastor Baker's final question about acceptance and forgiveness was really neat. What a super church!

Your brother,
Dan

And following is the last paragraph of a long letter I wrote to Dan and Sue in January 1984, expressing how much they'd meant to me over the years:

I am very thankful for your friendship, and wish you lived still in Portland, so we could see each other more often. I continue to thank God for bringing both of you into my life and using you to draw me closer to Himself. Although it's been over ten years ago now, I still remember you opening up your hearts and home to me on very short notice, and at times in the middle of the night, to talk with me, pray with me, weep with me, and rejoice with me, when I was feeling very weak, guilty, confused, and unlovable. When I hated myself, you loved me and kept on showing me that God's love is real, tangible, and constant.

With much love,
Jerry

The Retellings

Two months after giving my testimony at our church, I went even more public. Dr. Radmacher asked me to share my testimony with him on TV, on *The Gary Randall Show*. I accepted his invitation, and although I don't remember much of what I said, I do know that the segment aired on Portland's KOIN, channel 6, near the end of July 1980. We were all hoping and praying that God might use my testimony to provide help and hope to those needing it.

(Five years later, I would appear on the same TV show, again with Dr. Radmacher, this appearance associated with the 1985 release of Don Baker's book about me, *Beyond Rejection*. I was interviewed about the book, my testimony, and Rosie's and my ministry, called Reconciliation Ministry.)

Finally, in September 1980, I was able to return to Western Seminary in order to complete my last year of studies for my master of divinity degree. This was a great answer to prayer. But after a six-and-a-half-year break it was a big challenge to jump right back into the necessary level of intense study.

And God had more for me to do than just study. In fall 1979 Dr. Radmacher had asked me to share my testimony in chapel at the seminary. Rosie and I discussed it and prayed, and we declined at that time.

One year later I was back, and Dr. Radmacher repeated his request. We agreed.

This time was harder than sharing at Hinson. I was in almost daily contact with students, faculty, and staff. I did not know what to expect—how they would handle this. More specifically, I was not sure how I would handle seeing them every day, aware that they knew the dark, sinful side of me.

As the November 4 chapel service began, Dr. Radmacher started us out with the hymn, "Grace Greater Than Our Sin." I was seated on the platform with him, rising to the podium after he introduced me.

Within my first three sentences I revealed my life's greatest battle: "I have been a homosexual almost all my life." I briefly reviewed my history, up to the point of entering seminary and confiding in Dan Britts. I explained how my sin affected my sense of masculinity and how much I needed people to support me in my fight—a literal spiritual battle—to overcome my sin. But even in a place like this seminary I hadn't felt safe taking off my mask.

"I sat where you're sitting. I sat in the classrooms day after day, and my heart burned. I thought, *Oh God, where are you?*" I told about the bright spots, the nuggets of truth from God's Word, the friendships. "But there were so many days when I'd sit in class or sit here in chapel and want to jump up and say, 'Hey, who are we kidding? Why can't we take off these masks we're wearing? Why can't we say we're really hurting?'" I described homosexuality as "one of the most feared, most misunderstood things in our society," and I likened it to leprosy in the Bible. People with both conditions have been "treated as nonentities, nonhumans."

"I fought to keep this a secret," I said. "I thought this was necessary in order to continue living and having some sense of meaning and some self-image. So my standing up here and sharing is a tangible illustration of God's grace. Now I'm feeling the calmness and the liberty and the responsibility and the privilege of sharing what God can do, has done, and will do in people's lives."

I explained that the head knowledge I'd gained through three years of seminary was of only limited value until I experienced a lasting inner change. I recited how, in desperation, I'd finally confided in a few professors, and how I nearly took my own life. I told of the significant roles that individuals like Dan Britts, Don Baker, and Joel MacDonald had played in my gradual progress.

And I sang Rosie's praises. "I got married about five years ago by God's grace, and my Rosie has taught me, by her example, God's unconditional love and His total forgiveness, which did not seem humanly possible for this repeat offender. I had been unfaithful to my wife over and over in the first three years of our marriage. Yet she continued loving me, forgiving me, and crying out to God with me for victory."

And victory finally came! "The seeds of the victory began when I was in first grade," when I accepted Jesus Christ as Savior. And nothing had ever—nothing *could* ever—separate me from the love of God in Christ Jesus. Nothing! (Romans 8:1,31-39; John 10:28-29)

"For the past two years I've been enjoying victory over the practice of homosexuality. *To me, that's a miracle!* I attribute that totally to God. I kept saying to myself, 'Maybe this is an area that's just not possible to change. Maybe God is the God of the impossible for most things, but maybe not this.' But now my favorite verse is Luke 1:37: 'For with God nothing will be impossible.'" I repeated that promise: *"For with God nothing will be impossible.'* And He's proven that to me.

"I'm thankful for that victory, but God instructs us through Paul, 'In everything give thanks' (1 Thessalonians 5:18). 'Everything' includes the process. I can honestly thank God for allowing me for twenty-three years to battle this, because now I see that it has drawn me closer to God and to a total dependence on Him. It has taught me more of His character in the school of hard experiences, and I cling to His attributes daily. His unconditional love, His faithfulness, His longsuffering, His mercy, and His grace are beyond human description."

I shared samplings from my favorite chapter of the Bible, Psalm 30 in the *New International Version.* Verse 2: "O LORD my God, I called to you for help and you healed me." Verse 5: "His anger lasts only a moment, but His favor lasts a lifetime; weeping may remain for a night, but rejoicing comes in the morning." And verses 11-12, "You turned my wailing into dancing; you removed my sackcloth and clothed me with joy, that my heart may sing to you and not be silent. O LORD my God, I will give you thanks forever."

I dreamed out loud about the ministry opportunity arising out of my story—"the ministry that I've always desired if God ever should give me the victory. Throughout my years of struggling, I never had the opportunity of talking with someone who had had the victory in homosexuality. In the past several months God has given me a number of opportunities, publicly and individually, to *be* that person for others."

I challenged them to prayerfully consider their attitudes toward people struggling with this sin, and I left them with a list of practical pointers in ministering directly to such individuals:

- Be a good listener.
- Accept the person totally; love the sinner but hate the sin.
- Be a good friend; be available to talk anytime.
- Determine whether he or she is a Christian. If not, attempt to lead him or her to the Lord; otherwise, give him or her assurance.
- Emphasize regularly that change is possible (Luke 1:37).
- Determine whether the person definitely wants to change.
- Teach him or her the principles of confession, forgiveness, and restoration.
- Emphasize daily saturation with God's Word (Joshua 1:8; Romans 12:2; Philippians 4:8).
- Hold the person accountable for his or her actions.
- Most important, help him or her develop a strong, moment-by-moment dependence on God instead of just on humans.

"In conclusion," I concluded, "I don't know what battles each of you is facing, but I know that each of you struggles in some area of your life. I know that God can and will give you the victory in His perfect timing—perhaps not your timing, but in His. 'For with God nothing will be impossible!'

"Let's ask Him now for the impossible."

Life of the Married Student

What a great delight to be returning to seminary with a loving and supportive wife, who walked with me through that final year of studies. I was no longer alone, but was enjoying the companionship of the lady God had chosen for me. Being married as a full-time seminary student demanded that I make daily choices about how much time to spend studying and how much time to spend with Rosie. This was not always simple. Thankfully, Rosie was both understanding and supportive as I sought a healthy balance.

I also had to work part-time. During my first three years of seminary I received regular funds from the government, having served in the military. But now, typically three nights each week, I worked at a popular German restaurant called Der Rheinlander. I started as a busboy, then soon became a singing waiter. What fun to be able to work and sing in both German and English.

What a huge difference in my ability to concentrate on my studies and enjoy a more consistent walk with God, mainly because of my victory over my sexual struggles.

After publicly sharing my story at Hinson, I observed another big change in me. I was set free from what others thought of me. I no longer had to live in constant fear of others finding out about my sexual desires and sins. I realized I was enjoying a greater and greater level of liberating transparency with others. I no longer had to live in a prison of my own making, based on my fear of presumed rejection. And as I became more transparent with others, they in turn would often be more transparent with me. As I have often said, "Transparency breeds transparency," or at least invites it by way of example. My new openness was strong evidence of God's powerful, patient work of grace in my life.

Chapter 8

Reconciliation Ministry

To you, O Lord, I called; to the Lord I cried for mercy.
—King David, Psalm 30:8, NIV

He will my Shield and Portion be,
As long as life endures.

—John Newton, "Amazing Grace"

For many years—long before I experienced consistent victory in my struggle—I had a growing desire to offer hope and help to others who were also struggling with same-sex attraction. May 11, 1980, marked a turning point in my life and the inception of a new ministry for Rosie and me. My public disclosure at Hinson opened wide the door for increased awareness as well as the availability of hope and help.

Within churches there had long been a need for believers to become aware that, not only unbelievers, but also many believers are tempted by same-sex attraction. Heterosexual believers needed to become aware that there were many gay Christians, who were very unhappy and would like to change if it were possible. But with whom could they talk and receive understanding, love, and practical help? There were real risks involved with anyone wanting to help in this change process. One could be labeled "gay" merely by associating with people who were.

Remember, an estimated 50,000 people heard my testimony by radio broadcast on that critical Sunday. After that people began calling our church looking for help, and the church staff would in turn contact

Rosie and me. Then we would call the individuals or couples and set up times to meet with them in person, perhaps in our home, or their home, or at a neutral location like a restaurant. This went well for a while, but the requests started coming more frequently. Rosie and I both held full-time jobs, so we had limited time to meet individually with so many people. So about six months after my testimony we started a weekly support group, open to both men and women who struggled with homosexuality and wanted to overcome it. We began with eight or ten people, including Rosie and me, and grew at times to fifteen or twenty.

New people were always coming to our group. Sometimes they would decide to continue attending. Others might just come once or a few times and decide it was not for them, or not the right time. One ongoing challenge was how to effectively meet the widely differing needs of new people and regulars. But there were also benefits of a mixed, fluctuating group. The newcomers were often encouraged by the transparency and progress others were making. And when the regulars observed the fears, questions, doubts, shame, and guilt of the newer ones, they would be humbled by the memories of their recent condition. Also, they would often extend comfort, encouragement, hope, and prayers for the new people.

Our friends John and Laren Sloan assisted us with the group for two years, until they moved out of state. Neither of them had any past experience with homosexuality, but they both had loving, compassionate hearts for hurting, seeking people. What a wonderful addition they were to our support group, as they sought to come alongside individuals with Christ's love.

About two years after we had begun the weekly group for "strugglers," we also began a monthly support group for their family and friends. This was born out of a strong, unmet need among these confused and hurting people. We provided a safe, encouraging place where they could meet with others experiencing similar fears, concerns, doubts, questions, and dreams for their loved ones.

About this time Pastor Baker asked if he could write a book about Rosie and me, and we agreed. We met numerous times to interview, and he delved into my struggle with homosexuality and some of the measures that helped me walk in freedom and obedience to God. The book, *Beyond Rejection,* was released in June 1985, and we started receiving letters and calls in response. Within a year I was unable to reply to all the letters, some even from other countries. Most people assumed we had a full-time ministry.

Looking back now, I would have done many things differently. I wouldn't have offered my unrestricted availability. My model was Dan Britts, who was literally available to me day and night. Who was I, I reasoned, not to extend that same offer to anyone who might request my help? But that reasoning was naive and unrealistic. I was no superman; I needed time to eat and sleep. And Dan hadn't made that promise to everyone, only to me.

Pastor Jerry

Rosie and I both strongly wanted to go full-time with this ministry. We and others were praying that this would happen, but we lacked experience and funds. Finally we were given a boost of hope when Pastor Baker told me that the Hinson pastoral staff wanted me to join them as a full-time pastor, ministering to the gay community in the greater Portland area. He explained, however, that my hiring would need to be approved by the deacon board and by the church membership, which would take time.

We were elated. We began sharing the good news with friends and people involved with Reconciliation Ministry.

Sadly and surprisingly, a few months later I received a copy of a lengthy "Five Year Plan" prepared by the pastors. The final paragraph said something like: "With regard to Jerry Heacock and his proposed ministry to homosexuals, we are not making any recommendation at this time." We were disappointed and felt rejected and hurt, especially since the pastors had seemed so supportive of our ministry. I worked up the courage to ask for an explanation and was told that, upon further consideration, the pastors felt that Hinson Church was not yet ready for a major step like that. The idea was good, but the timing was not.

Eventually I was invited by a high-ranking government leader to talk with him about my testimony, our ministry, and the need in the Portland community. As a result of that meeting he invited pastors from numerous leading area churches to gather at his office. He asked me to share with them my testimony and vision for ministering to people affected by homosexuality in our community. The pastors all agreed that the problem was large and growing, and that something needed to be done. They felt that Portland could benefit from a ministry of this type. But nothing resulted from it, other than words of encouragement and more referrals of people to our ministry. No offers of help or funding were forthcoming.

We continued to volunteer our time and energy through Reconciliation Ministry, reaching out to more people. The growth was sporadic, yet real.

In our weekly support group we noticed issues that were common to many people, including fear, shame, guilt, hopelessness, and confusion. Many people were dealing with self-deception and deception by others—in other words, they believed lies and half-truths. And we dealt with a lot of curiosity: Who were we? What did we do? How long did the change process take?

People varied widely in their willingness to do the things required for healing and change. Some were only willing to do a limited amount within their comfort zones; others were willing to do almost anything in order to experience victory over their sexual temptations and behaviors. One example stands out in my memory. A young man in his late twenties or early thirties came to me feeling desperate and highly motivated. He had been thinking over Matthew 5:29-30, in which Jesus said, "If your right eye causes you to sin, pluck it out . . . . And if your right hand causes you to sin, cut it off." He thought it might be appropriate to be castrated in order to remove the urges and strong temptations. I told him I believed Jesus was using those strong images as *figurative* examples of our need to take sin seriously and to be willing to repent and make needed changes in our thinking and behavior. I explained that even if one removed his genitals, he would still deal with the thoughts and temptations that confront us constantly. In other words, *the main battle is in our minds.* He accepted that and decided not to take any drastic action.

Change Reconsidered

We launched our ministry with no book or program to follow—not even an example of another group like ours. Instead we learned as we went, by trial and error. We operated without any clear-cut understanding of the change process for gays. Theories abounded:

- The struggler needs more willpower.
- The struggler needs more knowledge—particularly by learning from God's Word.
- The struggler must deny fleshly desires.
- The struggler must have the "demon of homosexuality" cast out.
- The struggler only needs to "get saved" in order to change.

And more. Some raised the question, Is it even possible for gays to change, to be healed? And if so, how does one define, recognize, and verify "change" or "healing"?

We often discussed the benefits and risks of opening up with others about one's homosexual struggles. With whom should a gay person be open? And how open—partially or fully? Disclosure might lead to increased understanding, prayer support, encouragement, and accountability. It might open the gates to an inflow of compassion and acceptance, as in my experience. It could release one from fear of rejection, as well as from loneliness, knowing there is at least one companion on the journey toward freedom and victory. It leads to peace. Of course, rejection and ridicule are always possibilities. But if disclosure is handled correctly, we concluded that the benefits outweigh these risks.

In 1987, Rosie and I realized that working two full-time jobs plus investing in this ministry was causing us to neglect our relationship. So in the interest of carving out time for each other, we stepped away from Reconciliation Ministry. Since then I've been able to think further about my own change and healing process. I realize now that I was leading Reconciliation Ministry with some false assumptions, and I now understand the process more clearly. I was assuming that the struggler's needed change was limited to his or her sexuality, and that his or her biggest problem was homosexual sin. This implies that overcoming in this one area would make a person healthy and whole throughout his or her entire life.

Now that I've experienced additional change, growth, and healing in my life, I realize how narrow this thinking was. Instead of focusing on one sin or one aspect of a person's makeup, the most effective approach targets the person's entire being—all aspects of health and maturity, including thoughts, attitudes, and actions in all areas of life. *The primary goal isn't just sexual healing—it's whole-person healing and maturing, also known as sanctification.*

The answer is not simply "salvation" in the sense of becoming a child of God by grace through personal faith in Jesus Christ, although this relationship with Jesus is certainly the foundation. Being a Christian does not guarantee automatic victory over this sin, as I witnessed for more than thirty years. Nor is the answer simply a matter of becoming consistently obedient to God in this one area. Rather the goal needs to be viewed as the complete process of sanctification that begins when a person becomes a believer and continues throughout the rest of his or her life on earth.

I think 2 Corinthians 3:18 is an excellent verse that describes this process of sanctification: "We all, with unveiled face, beholding as in a mirror the glory of the Lord, are being transformed into the same image from glory to glory, just as by the Spirit of the Lord."

At first I was focused on just this one struggle, so out of ignorance I was teaching and guiding others to think mainly of their sexuality. But what about other areas of sin—dishonesty, hostility, hurtful words, and so on? And even more important, consider the goals of true maturity: love, joy, peace, patience, and the rest of the fruit of the Spirit (Galatians 5:22-23).

Fortunately, our ministry has matured in the time since we stepped aside from it in May 1987. It is now known as The Portland Fellowship and has incorporated as a nonprofit organization. Over these many years I have periodically returned to visit, to speak, to lead a monthly support group for family and friends, and to participate in a smaller alumni group. I have been greatly encouraged to witness how this ministry has grown and broadened to more effectively meet the needs of a much larger group of people. The leadership has provided the necessary vision, structure, and heart for God, and He continues using them and this ministry in remarkable ways.

To God be the glory. Great things He has done!

Chapter 9

Maturing Years

"What gain is there in my destruction, in my going down into the pit?
Will the dust praise you? Will it proclaim your faithfulness?"

—King David, Psalm 30:9, NIV

Yea, when this flesh and heart shall fail,
And mortal life shall cease,

—John Newton, "Amazing Grace"

When I found myself suddenly leading a ministry to gays and their families, I began looking around for anyone else from whom I might learn. In June 1981 I attended the weeklong EXODUS VI, an annual conference on ministry to homosexuals. It proved informative, challenging, and encouraging. Then over the summer I contacted Frank Worthen of Love in Action and Barbara Johnson of Spatula Ministries—two California ministries to gays and their families—asking about the possibilities of interning with them for a period of weeks. Both agreed enthusiastically. With financial help from Hinson and several of our friends, I spent six weeks in California, most of it with Love in Action. Rosie joined me for the last two weeks.

In this training opportunity I did general office work, participated in group meetings and Bible studies, resided in the live-in community house, took part in all the activities of the residential program, learned how to set up a ministry office, prepared newsletters, and much more. I was unspeakably grateful for this excellent, unique, and specific training as I developed Reconciliation Ministry.

The early 1980s involved a lot of flux in my work life. I worked a year in rental property management for two men I knew—a big challenge but a very good learning and broadening experience. Eventually I got back into insurance sales, first with LTH and Associates, a small agency where I found it refreshing to broker sales through a variety of companies, instead of only one.

Pain in the Neck

About this time I noticed a bump on my neck, but did not think much of it and forgot about it. Then it kept growing and a year later I commented to Rosie about it. She insisted I have it checked, so I did. I was told I had a tumor in my left salivary gland and should have it removed.

I must admit I was a bit scared, as I was told the tumor might be cancerous. Also, I was told that even if the tumor was benign, the large facial nerve could be damaged or severed and the entire left side of my face might permanently droop. Was I ever thankful to be able to turn to God and trust Him for the outcome!

The day before my surgery, I was thinking very soberly because of the slight possibility that I may not survive the surgery, due to standard risks of any surgery. So I made a point to talk with my parents, as well as Dan Britts, Joel MacDonald, and John Sloan.

The hour of the surgery arrived on September 20, 1984, and at my request the surgical team held off anesthetizing me until I could pray with them. Once I'd prayed—the lady surgeon holding my hand—an amazing peace came over me; I knew that God was present and that He would oversee the operation.

That night I wrote, "Without a doubt I knew of God's presence with me moment by moment today. I rejoiced in being able to experience God's presence and strength and help in so many ways today. I prayed with Rosie in the car before going in the hospital and claimed Isaiah 41:10."

My wonderful surgeon gave me the good news that my neck tumor was benign, and there were no complications during surgery. What a huge relief. My heart was filled with gratitude to God for His answer to our prayers.

It's the Mailman!

Shortly after my surgery I quit my insurance sales job. That left me looking for the next step along God's path for me.

If you had asked me when I was growing up if I wanted to become a mailman, I would have said no. It never entered my mind as even a remote interest. But after the preceding several years of futile job juggling, I was open to try almost anything. I found out the pay and benefits were good in the Postal Service. And I would start off the first year with four weeks' vacation because my four years of active duty with the Army counted toward my years of federal service employment. So I applied.

I started my new job at the East Portland Station in April 1985 and worked six years as a "letter carrier" (although *mailman* is the title I preferred), until I resigned to begin working as a full-time chaplain starting April 1, 1991.

I liked the good pay and benefits, the three-day weekends every six weeks, the exercise walking, and being outside in good weather. It was fun getting to know some of my fellow letter carriers. We would tease and encourage each other often.

One of my favorite aspects was interacting with my customers. Often customers would meet me at their door or in the yard and say, "Don't give me any junk mail today." They usually responded with a laugh when I'd reply, "It's not junk mail, it's job mail!" When customers had serious health issues, or maybe a death in the family, I would sometimes pray for them at their doorstep or even visit them in the hospital.

I enjoyed the standing offers from customers for hot or cold beverages. I remember one very cold winter morning with snow, ice, and heavy winds. As I began my route near the top of Mount Tabor, I became chilled and extremely discouraged after only walking a few blocks. *I can't do this all day,* I thought. About then a retired couple met me at their door, invited me inside to warm up by the fireplace, and gave me hot coffee and cookies. That simple act of kindness warmed me so much, both inside and out, that I found the strength to work all day and finish my route.

During my first year and a half I substituted for letter carriers who were sick or on vacation, so I didn't have regular customers. But for my last four and a half years I had my own regular route on the northeast slope of Mount Tabor. I enjoyed getting to know the people—many of them retirees—as well as their dogs. Some gradually moved into Baptist Manor, a large retirement and nursing home where I would later serve as chaplain. Rosie and I still keep in touch with several former customers more than twenty years later.

The job had its share of frustrations. I didn't enjoy the repetition involved in each day's work. I missed getting to use my seminary training. The outdoors weren't so friendly when the bad weather hit. The physical work sometimes took a toll on my body; I developed carpal tunnel syndrome, which improved after I left postal work. And I felt the stress of constant pressure from supervisors to speed up. I was always being timed, for both inside and outside work, but my mind would easily wander while sorting mail, and I hated rushing my time with customers on my route.

I sometimes found myself mentally "wrestling" with God over the way my life was going, contrary to my wishes and prayers. I also sometimes struggled against sexual fantasies in my thought life because of the boredom of the job; the sexually provocative materials in the mail didn't help. Fortunately, more often than not these challenges led me to pray more.

I often felt like a failure, since I could not consistently meet the expectations of postal management. But at the same time I felt I was succeeding by providing a good income for Rosie.

Making Headlines

If you lived in the Vancouver, Washington, area on Sunday, May 18, 1986, and you subscribed to the main Vancouver newspaper, *The Columbian,* and if you opened up the newspaper to the front page of the "View" section, you would have been treated to a large photo of Rosie and me seated and facing one another. Taking up most of the page and one column of the next page were two articles about us and our ministry, spanned by the overarching headline, "Gays seek change through religion," both written by Wendy Reif.

Both articles were well written and did a good job of quoting us accurately. The first article had its own headline, "Homosexuality seen as conquerable sin," and began with these thought-provoking words:

> "Get straight in 10 easy lessons" might be a flashy message Jerry Heacock could use to get people interested in his ministry to gays.
>
> In a society that boasts cures for alcoholism in 10-day sessions and drastic weight loss in 30 days, perhaps gays looking to change their sexual orientation might think there would be a fast cure.

It went on to say: "There is no guarantee offered nor statistics quoted on their chances of succeeding. Speaking 'tongue in cheek,' Heacock said the cure rate is '100 percent for those who honestly want to change based on God's word.'"

The other article was headlined, "Gay 'went public' before congregation." Beneath the photo of me and Rosie was a caption quoting me: "Homosexuality is learned behavior . . . To me, the bottom line is that they're actually saying, 'I don't want to accept the responsibility of change.'"

I wish an article like this had run in the main Portland newspaper, *The Oregonian*. This type of article would most likely not be printed in our papers today. So many changes have occurred over the past three decades.

Malana

On Pearl Harbor Day 1990 my family experienced our own major tragedy.

My sister, Collette, had only one child—her daughter, Malana. What a cute, sweet, vivacious little girl. She was my parents' only living grandchild.

Tragically, Malana contracted leukemia at age twelve and died on December 7, shortly before her thirteenth birthday. Our whole family felt this loss and grieved deeply. My heart ached for Collette as she struggled to continue on without her daughter.

Time can help heal even the most grievous of wounds, and now both Collette and we look forward to being with Malana again, forever in heaven.

At the time I didn't realize that I was mere months away from beginning a career in which I would deal with death and dying on a daily basis.

Malana at twelve

Chapter 10

Rejoicing Years

"Hear, O LORD, and be merciful to me; O LORD, be my help."
—King David, Psalm 30:10, NIV

I shall possess, within the veil,
A life of joy and peace.

—John Newton, "Amazing Grace"

"What's a chaplain do?" many people have asked over the years. In the US Army I learned firsthand what military chaplains do and what a unique and wonderful service they provide. Little did I know then that I would become a chaplain myself.

Without warning, my heart and mind began sensing a strong pull in an unexpected direction in fall 1990. Rosie and I were in a Sunday morning worship service at Lynch Baptist Church, listening to a guest speaker named Ray Holder, chaplain at Tuality Hospital in Hillsboro, Oregon. As he shared some of his responsibilities and experiences, I began to feel drawn toward that ministry. He spoke of coming alongside patients and their hurting families, who needed someone to listen and share their pain. The more Chaplain Holder spoke, the more I could see myself doing what he was doing. I was anxious to find out what Rosie thought about the idea of me becoming a chaplain. To my delight, she said she could easily see me doing that type of work.

We talked about it for a few weeks, and I called Chaplain Holder to ask him what was necessary to become a chaplain. He answered my questions and referred me to Chaplain Tim Malyon, who both served as a Portland hospital chaplain and oversaw numerous chaplains as the area director with HCMA (Hospital Chaplains Ministry of America). After I had talked with Chaplain Malyon several times, he encouraged me to apply with HCMA.

But I would need to resign from the post office and give up a good salary and very good benefits. Instead I would need to raise financial and prayer support from individuals and churches. In faith and with Rosie's agreement, I applied. After a variety of interviews, I was accepted and began my work as a chaplain on April 1, 1991. I was selected to be the chaplain at Baptist Manor in Portland, a large retirement and nursing home with about 180 residents and over a hundred staff.

Chaplain Heacock

When someone calls for a chaplain, 'tis music to my ears.
When He calls, may I quickly reply, "Here am I! Send me."
—Jerry Heacock (see Isaiah 6:8)

At time of this writing I've been serving as a chaplain for twenty-four years—sometimes part-time, at times taking breaks for critical life events. In all that time I've been self-employed as an independent contractor of my services. (Most of the chaplains I know work on this same basis.) Most of my financial support has been provided by donations from individuals and, at times, churches. The funds all go through the organization with which I am affiliated, originally through HCMA, and since fall 1998 through NHM (Nursing Home Ministries). At times a facility where I'm serving will contribute a small but regular donation to help with my support.

At Baptist Manor I started at four hundred dollars per month for three days' work a week. The other two days I went through an intense chaplain internship program, working at four Portland area hospitals. After nine months, I became full-time at Baptist Manor. Even then I had to work to get an increase, which was gradually granted over the following six years. During the last of those years they paid me nine hundred dollars per month with no benefits, and I averaged fifty hours per week. I prepared for and conducted three worship services in a row each Sunday, and three Bible studies every week. It was like preparing for three different congregations. I give credit to God, because on my own I couldn't have done everything expected of me.

In the process of applying to go full-time at Baptist Manor, evaluators learned that I'd previously lived the gay lifestyle. The main decision maker got a copy of Don Baker's book, *Beyond Rejection,* read it, and seemed satisfied with my testimony. But he wanted to discuss the hiring decision with the Baptist Manor board of directors. I consented. The board then interviewed—no, *interrogated*—me about my past and how I was doing in the present. It was embarrassing, but they expressed faith that I was living in freedom and victory and so decided to bring me on as chaplain.

I can't help but wonder if they would have done this for other types of past sinful behavior. Or was their response unique to this sensitive issue, which is often misunderstood?

I was more fully devoted to this job than to anything ever before. I was available twenty-four hours a day, seven days a week. I wanted to know *now* if someone had died or was dying, in order to do my job. If the dying person is alert and alone, they need someone there to comfort and pray. If family or friends are there, they also need support. And I know a death affects the facility staff—some deeply—and it's my privilege to support them.

God has hardwired me to go into any situation and be God's hands and voice to the hurting. All of the traumatic events that Rosie and I have gone through simply make me more sensitive to what others are going through. Second Corinthians 1:3-4 sums up the chaplaincy: "Blessed be . . . the Father of mercies and God of all comfort, who comforts us in all our tribulation, that we may be able to comfort those who are in any trouble, with the comfort with which we ourselves are comforted by God." Chaplains come alongside, not to lecture or preach, but to bring my "three words"—love, presence, and listening. Not because it's our job, but because the love of Christ flows through us. Chaplain Tim Malyon taught me *the ministry of presence* both by precept and even more by his example.

Long before I started as a chaplain, God decided what gifts and abilities I would need for this job. He had been gradually preparing me for more than twenty years. He used my experience as a chaplain's assistant in the Army. Through my experience in insurance sales He cultivated my heart for the needs of others. As a letter carrier I had countless opportunities to encourage, to comfort, to listen, to be compassionately present, and to love.

Throughout school and as a singing waiter I cultivated the gift of music, which has become an important part of my ministry. I have music in my veins. I loved Baptist Manor, where they had pianos all over the facility. One facility more recently said they'd welcome me whenever I can come to play the piano and lead residents in singing. They would fit their schedule around me.

I enjoy chaplaincy so much because I have the freedom that God wants me to have. I get the challenge of being creative, the opportunity to meet and care for lots of people, and the freedom of making my own hours. One thing I really like is putting together programs for Christmas or Easter or Thanksgiving, involving as many residents and staff as possible. I've used music and drama, written my own scripts, recruited actors and musicians, and delegated various tasks.

For one Christmas pageant, Mary and Joseph were each one hundred years old. When I first attempted to recruit my "Mary," she read the script to consider it. She came back a few days later and said, "I can't do this. I'm too old to have a baby. People will laugh." I reminded her of Sarah, to whom God gave a baby in her old age. She still resisted. Finally she acknowledged, "I'd be willing to do it if I can change some of the wording." I readily agreed. People talked about it long afterward, asking, "When can we do something like that again?"

Some people ask, "How do you handle all the death?" The truth is, I'd rather do a funeral than a wedding. What a large responsibility and privilege to be invited into a family's home and walk with them through the early stages of the grieving process. Ecclesiastes 7:3-4 says of times like this, "Sorrow is better than laughter, for by a sad countenance the heart is made better. The heart of the wise is in the house of mourning." And there is "a time to weep, and a time to laugh; a time to mourn, and a time to dance" (Ecclesiastes 3:4). I'm designed by God to help people through the times of weeping and mourning.

I now have to limit my availability and watch for burnout. It's hard for me to say no. I see the need, and I want to help. But I can't give my best to the most strategic needs if I'm available day and night. At time of this writing I'm spreading myself between four facilities and writing my book.

Over and over again people in various care facilities open up their lives to me. They seem to feel safe trusting me with things they would tell nobody else. Now and then, while working full-time at Baptist Manor, I would start feeling very weighed down, as if trying to carry everyone's burdens on my back. One sweet, godly lady said to me, "Chaplain, all of our problems are far too much for you to carry yourself. You need to keep handing them over to God. He can handle them." I've often needed to remember and apply that.

Ordination

In the fall of 1991, as I was going through the ordination process, my homosexual past became an issue again. I had written out my statement of faith and my Christian testimony and did not mention my struggle with homosexuality. I was informed that I needed to include it and not appear as though I was trying to hide it. This surprised me, since for more than a decade I'd been very public about my past through the media, through my public testimony, and in my leadership of Reconciliation Ministry. But I willingly added a description of my past struggles and victory, which was well received.

Again, though, I wondered if this request would have been made if the issue were some other type of sin. The stereotypes and stigma of homosexuality are not easy to overcome in people's minds. As I reflect on the ordination process now, I am grateful they took it seriously enough to ask me about this past struggle and whether or not I was still living in freedom from it. They were diligently seeking to ordain men to Christian ministry who respected sexual purity, not only in word, but in deed. Though it was awkward for both them and me at the time, it was vitally important.

The ordination ceremony itself was like another "coming out" for me. At this time Rosie and I were attending Lynch Baptist Church. My official ordination would take place before the congregation, and one of the speakers was to be Don Baker. At the last minute, Pastor Baker came to me and asked, "Do the people here know about your history?"

"No," I answered. This had been something of a fresh start for Rosie and me.

"Oh," he said, taken a little aback. "I was planning to mention how far you've come and the book about you. I guess I'd better talk to the pastor first."

Apparently the pastor consented, and once again I found myself "standing naked," exposed before another roomful of Christians, wondering how they would respond. I need not have feared; I found acceptance. Pastor Baker had nothing but good to say about me and the Lord's work in my life. He highlighted the uniqueness of this event and how difficult it is for those who struggle with same-sex attraction to leave that lifestyle behind. For the ordination board to express enough confidence to endorse me for Christian ministry was a huge testimony to God's life-changing power.

It was a landmark day for me. For years—even after I had ceased my homosexual behavior in 1978—I had still been trudging through life, assuming I was washed up, useless to the Lord for His original purpose. I was resigned to make the best of a ruined existence, never daring even to dream that I might actually get to serve Him in ministry. I can't find words to express the new hope I felt when the dream became reality. Not only had the Lord rescued me *from* my past; in some ways I was better equipped for ministry *because of* my past.

This freedom reminds me of seagulls. I've always admired their beauty in flight—so seemingly effortless, soaring on the wind. I've always wanted the freedom they represent, rather than being limited to walking on the ground.

I once sat at my piano playing the tune to "Danny Boy," and I started making up new words to go with the tune:

Oh, Jesus Christ, You are my Lord and Savior.
You love me more than words can ever tell...

On I sang, swelling at the end with

Oh, Jesus, let me soar once with the seagulls,
And then I'll know, I'll know just how to fly!

I'm still learning how to fly. But on the day of my ordination the Lord taught me one of my greatest lessons in freedom.

Birthday Cards

In the weeks leading up to my fiftieth birthday—January 8, 1995—my dear, sweet Rosie contacted many of my friends and invited them to write birthday notes to me. Following are a few excerpts.

From Phil Hobizal (a long-time friend, to whom I handed leadership of Reconciliation Ministry in 1987):

> It's hard for me to believe that a guy with as much energy and enthusiasm as you is fifty years old. . . .
>
> God has entrusted you with the special task of caring for His aging children. I believe the tenderness of your heart and your unveiled faith in Christ make you the perfect shepherd at the Baptist Manor. I'd like to underline two character qualities I've experienced in you which have been a blessing to me and my family.
>
> The first is joy. You, my friend, have a bubbly personality that affects those around you. That is a fruit of the Spirit of God working through you to all our benefit. From the first time I heard you singing "Cheer Ye Up Ye Saints of God" at a Reconciliation meeting, I was convinced that you were going to face adversities with an attitude of praise and thanksgiving. Thanks for displaying your belief that "with God, all things are possible."
>
> The second is faithfulness. You have proved over the years that you are willing to lay down your desires to do God's will. When Rosie needed you years ago, you were willing to give up your own personal goals to take care of your wife. That is honorable. Choosing to do what was right rather than pursue ministry reminds me of Jesus' words: "Not my will, but yours be done."

From Roger Larson (fellow seminary student and pianist):

> You helped me through a very difficult chapter in my life and always let me know you cared. The dinners

with you and Rosie were such an encouragement. I
remember lots of laughter as well as good talks.

From Bill Heck (fellow seminary student, speaker at my ordination):

> Jerry, there are a number of qualities that I have seen
> in you, admired in you, of which I have been on the
> receiving end. You are a loyal and faithful friend. . . .
>
> You are also a sensitive man, and I respect that in
> you immensely. You have a God-given ability to feel
> what other people are feeling and to assure them that
> what they are feeling matters to you. You have tremen-
> dous insight into the hearts and lives of those around
> you. This quality is teamed up with a good ability to
> listen to others. I get the impression that you have
> really heard me when I talk with you. That is a rare
> and unique gift that you bring to your relationships.
>
> Jerry, you are a person who enjoys life, and finds
> delight in every moment.

From Dan Britts:

> I want to thank you for being a special friend and
> being the initiative taker in keeping us in touch.
> Maintaining long-term or even close short-time
> friendships is not a strong suit for me and I appre-
> ciate you hanging in there with me.
>
> I hope you enjoy your big day and one day if we
> both can remain injury-free, let's run a marathon
> together.

From Pastor Don Richter (from the weekly Portland pastors prayer
group, now with Jesus in heaven):

> Friendly, encouraging, willing worker, thoughtful,
> bilingual, helpful, and hospitable. And I add that you

make any good conversation both stimulating and better. Thank you for being you and enriching my life.

From Chaplain Tim Malyon (my first chaplaincy mentor, now with the Lord):

> God has blessed you with an enthusiasm for life which I have always appreciated. I pray that will never be diminished by the passing of years. . . . Because of this wonderful trait, the Lord allows you to lift the spirits of those around you. That coupled with your compassion for others, plus your theological orientation, makes you a special instrument whom God is using effectively in the chaplaincy. . . . He has given you real joy and blessing as you have faithfully ministered at Baptist Manor. I commend you, my good brother.
>
> And be good to Rosie. She is your finest asset, other than the Lord.

From Dave (college housemate):

> Looking back at the days we spent together now so many years ago, I am drawn to the instant rapport we had both on a personal and spiritual level that has sustained our friendship over the years. We had great fun living at His House while attending the UO [University of Oregon], sometimes staying up all night to solve the issues confronting us as young adults ready to take our place in the world.

From Dr. Crosby Englizian:

> When I think of Jerry Heacock, I recall a troubled young man who was courageous enough to become vulnerable and to humble himself before his teachers, and to do what was suggested as an avenue toward long-term mental and spiritual health.

This you have done with alacrity and perseverance. You have made a new life for yourself—with
Rosie—and with a meaningful and useful ministry.
You are surely to be commended for the progress
which has been made over rough terrain.

Part of a poem my father wrote for me:

> Not a mean bone in his body
> Nothing but love in his heart.
> His thoughts always for others
> From morning, noon and till dark.
>
> Ever since he was a little lad
> He has ever looked to the Lord,
> Always studying, memorizing, and reading
> Checking out all of God's Word!

From Dr. Robert Cook:

> As I think about you perhaps the thing that most
> captivates me is your loving pastoral care for those to
> whom God has called you to minister. I feel strongly
> that the Lord has definitely led you into your cur-
> rent special ministry and it makes my heart rejoice to
> think of this joining of your gifts and the real needs
> of the folk to whom you minister.

A Visit to India

Rosie and I tried to ensure that we extended God's compassion, not only to those near us, but also to those afar. From 1985
to 1995 we sponsored a young Indian man named Krupa through
Compassion International. I had been praying throughout those ten
years that someday I might be able to go to India and meet Krupa
in person.

Krupa at twenty

The answer to my prayers came when I was invited to go with an Indian evangelist on a mission trip with a group of pastors to Southern India. Rosie decided not to go, but she strongly encouraged me to go.

So I did, for three weeks in May and June 1995.

I'd never been in a country with such deep poverty and so much diversity. The city of Madras (now called Chennai) had about ten million people. The streets were filled with buses, cars, bikes, bicycle-taxis, ox-drawn carts, and all manner of other modes of transport. We arrived during what we were told was record-breaking heat, not to mention humidity.

We so easily take drinking water for granted here in the US. In India we were told to drink only bottled water, and even to be careful that it was indeed safely bottled and sealed. This struck me so powerfully that I brought home a bottle of water as a souvenir. (About a year later Rosie saw it and emptied out the water, thinking I merely wanted to save the container. Oops!)

I enjoyed the wide variety of foods and spices. I also learned to enjoy eating most foods with my fingers, as was the custom. And I came to like very much both the aroma and spicy taste of *chai,* the Indian version of tea.

The crusade for which we'd come was held in Karaikudi, a city of 300,000 along the coast in Southern India. It lasted six nights, plus outdoor baptisms on Sunday morning at the end. I spoke briefly one evening of the crusade and sang a solo, "I'd Rather Have Jesus." I also taught during the daytimes with an interpreter, particularly on the topic of Scripture memory and meditation. The evangelist who led the team described me as the team "cheerleader."

One of our team members was a man whom we'll call James (not his real name). His brother, Paul (also a pseudonym), had just graduated from a college in central India and joined us during the week of the crusade to be with his brother. Paul was a strong Hindu, but I had the immense privilege of leading him to Christ, along with the help and prayers of James. His was a unique and dramatic conversion. This was the first time I had so clearly seen the enemy's power. It was so strong that Paul could not at first say the name of Jesus.

After he prayed to receive Jesus as his Savior, he insisted I stay with him and his brother in their hotel room. He was feeling anxious about what evil spirits might do to him. James dismissed the request, but Paul kept on pleading. I finally consented; I got my pillow and a few things out of my room and settled in with them. Various times during the night, Paul would awaken and feel troubled and attacked by evil spirits. He would awaken us and ask us to pray for him. Finally, we told him he could pray himself and tell God his concerns and ask God for help. We told him that he could pray for the blood of Jesus to cover him when he was feeling attacked, just as we had been praying. It was such a delight to hear him saying brief prayers during the night, ending them "in the name of the Jesus Christ." I likened his beginning prayers to a young child learning to talk. This brother's early, earnest prayers must have brought much joy to our Father in heaven.

We all rejoiced when Paul shared his testimony during the final night of the crusade. I also had the joy of helping with his baptism that Sunday. On our way there Paul shared that during the night he had had nightmares in which demons were threatening to kill his parents and cause him to drown if he was baptized. James reassured him that God is all-powerful and could easily handle any demons coming against him or his family.

Several years later I heard that Paul had been visiting various villages in Southern India, sharing Jesus with others!

I am grateful to the Compassion International office in Madras. They helped coordinate Krupa's and his father's train travel to attend the crusade. And when I went with them to their village, Compassion International provided an interpreter for the trip.

How clearly I can picture the first time I saw Krupa and his father, Pastor Joshua, at the train station. I recognized them from photos Krupa had sent me. What joy flooded over me as I shook Krupa's and his father's hands and we hugged for the very first time! Another dream come true.

At the conclusion of the crusade, Krupa, his father, and I traveled three days by train and then by rental car over rough, mostly dirt roads—around the occasional water buffalo—to their small village of Meduru. When we reached the edge of the village, I thought I heard music. It was a small group of villagers enthusiastically playing various instruments as they welcomed us and paraded us through the village. Most villagers lived in small, thatch-roofed huts. People of all ages streamed from their huts and followed us as we wound our way through the village. Finally the band stopped playing, the car stopped, and we arrived at the church building where Pastor Joshua served. Above the dirt road hung a large banner that said in bold letters: "Welcome Mr. Jerry W. Heacock." What a surprise to see my name displayed in the middle of an Indian village!

A number of villagers came up and began putting heavy floral leis over my head—three of them. Krupa invited me to speak to the children and youth of the village inside the church, and he interpreted.

I had taken some gifts for Krupa and his family and had fun distributing those. I was surprised to find that Krupa's family lived in a very small area inside the church, merely sectioned off with curtains. They provided a large meal in my honor, for which I sensed they had sacrificed.

Later that afternoon I felt weary from the intense heat, the travel, and the emotional impact of events. The interpreter and I lay down on special mats and napped, while several young people stood fanning us with large palm branches. (I asked Rosie to do this for me back home; she was less obliging.)

Krupa, his sister and parents

It was hard to say goodbye to Krupa and his father as they saw me off at the train station. We all knew that we might never see one another again this side of heaven. *I left part of my heart with them, and with the people of India.* I would have loved to stay longer. How I wished Rosie could have been there with me.

It was a long, lonely trip for me on the train returning to Madras.

I had heard of culture shock, but I don't know if I had ever heard of *reverse* culture shock. Rosie picked me up at the Portland airport and drove us back home. When she turned onto our street, I caught sight of our large, modern Victorian home, which we had had custom built six years before. Suddenly I asked Rosie to pull the car over and stop. I sat speechless, struggling to put into words what I was feeling. I slowly asked Rosie: "Is that our home?" Scenes from the streets of India flashed before my mind—especially the dirt "streets" in Krupa's village, lined with small, thatched huts. The stark contrast was almost more than I could grasp. I could not help but think of the millions of people in India who are homeless or living in extreme poverty.

Krupa and I have stayed in touch by letter and phone. Three years after visiting India, I learned that Krupa's father had died suddenly and unexpectedly. In God's timing, Krupa had just graduated from Bible college and was back home. Krupa was thus equipped to step into his father's shoes and pastor the churches in the villages that his father had been shepherding.

More years passed and Krupa married and began having children. With our permission they named their first child Rosie, though they had never met my wife. They called and asked us to name their second child, a daughter, and we chose Elizabeth Grace. Later Krupa called saying they were expecting another child, a boy, and asked us to name him. After thinking and praying it over, we suggested Joshua, after Krupa's father.

He liked that, but paused and added, "But we like your name also."

So I said, "Then call him Joshua Jerry."

So they did. Their fourth child is a daughter they named Siri.

A few weeks after returning home I was still trying to process the vast differences between the US and India. I asked Rosie what she would think of selling our home and moving to India to serve God there for the rest of our lives. To my surprise she said she would be willing to do that! I'm so proud of her.

Unfortunately, life circumstances would intervene over the following years that would make it impossible for us to live and serve in India. That was apparently not part of God's plan for us.

I wish it were possible to take Rosie with me to India to meet Krupa and his family, and to share my experiences. Will I ever go back? At times I have thought I would like to take a short-term missions team there. Only God knows what may happen in the future.

Rosie's Weight Struggle

In our American culture one's body weight and size carries significance far beyond what it deserves. These measures should not determine a person's value as a human created in God's image. Sadly, many tend to criticize and reject others who are "too skinny" or "too fat."

I grew up, like so many, very aware of other people's size. From childhood I would hear countless unkind remarks and labels used especially to describe overweight people. As a consequence I grew up thinking and dreaming about eventually marrying a lovely young lady who was petite. Then Rosie came into my life and my thinking gradually changed for the better. As my love for her grew and I saw deeper into her spirit, her weight became less and less of an obstacle to me.

We married in July 1975 and I began to know Rosie for the first time in a sexually intimate way. At times her weight was an problem for me, when I found myself comparing her to my fantasy of a woman's ideal size. Her weight changed often over our first twenty-two years of marriage. She would gain and then lose and then gain again. By December 1995 she had more than doubled her weight as a bride. She weighed 426 pounds and looked so vastly different that she did not appear to be the same lady I married. Actually, she was not the same woman I had married. *On the inside, she was far better!*

Rosie before surgery

Rosie's weight was merely one of many factors I struggled with in our relationship. Another major factor had to do with the countless memories of gay fantasies and experiences I had had over the years, including the first three years of our marriage. I would try to forget them, but found it very difficult.

In December 1995, Rosie had a "dystal gastric bypass" (a specific type of "stomach stapling"). She proved to be an ideal patient, following all of her surgeon's guidance. Prior to her surgery she could only walk about one block without stopping to rest. Before long she could walk one or two miles. Then gradually she increased to walking six or eight miles with me on some Saturdays. Then she would want to hurry home to clean house and work outside in the flowerbeds or go grocery shopping. *She lost about three hundred pounds in just less than two years!* Many people who had tried to get Rosie to lose weight began telling her she was too skinny and needed to eat more.

For several reasons I was becoming more and more excited for her and for us. I became more sexually attracted to her. I looked forward to doing activities together that we'd been unable to do before—swimming, walking, riding bikes, maybe even running together.

Looking back from my vantage point today, I see that period as a window of a few years, during which God was allowing us a glimpse of what she'll look like in heaven. Traumatic circumstances, about which you will read in the coming chapters, changed our lives dramatically, and after a few years Rosie started gaining weight again. Today she has gained back about half of what she had lost.

Glimpse of heaven, 1998

Our plans and dreams and goals were silenced for a time. Yet God was not silent, nor was He indifferent. Rather, God began revealing Himself to both of us in new ways. He slowed us down and enabled us to hear His voice more clearly and to observe His loving actions through countless people.

I am overweight myself and am trying to lose about twenty-five pounds. Rosie is working on losing also and is having some encouraging success.

I can truthfully say that I have loved Rosie through thick and thin. No matter her size, Rosie is a wonderful, loving, incredible person, to whom I am blessed to be married. Rosie and I are indeed soul mates and best friends. She is my "Mrs. Wonderful" and my "Schatzi" (literally "treasure," equivalent to the English "sweetheart").

Chapter 11

Traumatic Years

You turned my wailing into dancing; you removed my sackcloth and clothed me with joy, that my heart may sing to you and not be silent.
> —King David, Psalm 30:11-12, NIV

The earth shall soon dissolve like snow,
The sun forbear to shine;
> —John Newton, "Amazing Grace"

*I*n January 1996 I attended the four-day Portland Pastor's Prayer Summit—an annual event held at the Cannon Beach Conference Center, attended this year by a hundred men, some of whom I knew very well. According to my journal I went praying that God would "open my ears and heart these four days to listen clearly to You."

On the third day—a Wednesday—the Lord brought to my conscious mind a trauma from my past that I had relegated to a dull, subconscious ache for more than eighteen years. It was Rosie's miscarriage just before Christmas 1977. The loss of our child . . . *or children,* I always mentally add, since it's possible that God had given us the twins for which we had often prayed.

That afternoon I brought it up in the prayer meeting with the other pastors, explaining that I had never been able to grieve properly after losing our only child. I was beginning to realize that for all those years I had been carrying a burden of pain and loss and anger toward God. I told my friends that I needed to accept God's perfect timing and to stop blaming Him, as if He had made a mistake.

They invited me to sit in a chair placed in the center of the room and they prayed for me, many standing and kneeling around me with their hands on my shoulders and head. One in particular, Bob Powell, knelt directly in front of me and was very sensitive to what was happening in me. He quietly repeated encouragement to "release it" and "let it come out" and "it's okay." Finally, the pain came up and out in deep sobs that I allowed myself to stop controlling.

"Thank you, Father," I wrote later in my journal, "for releasing me from that deep and heavy pain and for helping me to accept Your perfect timing in taking our unborn children to be with You. I thank You for renewing and strengthening my hope to see our child (or children) eventually in heaven and to anticipate being with them forever! Thank You, Father, for the many hugs and comforting words from my fellow pastors. Their arms were like a tangible extension of Your arms, Lord. Tonight during and after communion I was struck in a new and deeper way with the truth that You lost Your Son, Your only Son, through death also."

Thursday afternoon and evening, after I returned home, I debriefed at length with Rosie. She, as usual, listened patiently and well, and appreciated the prayers of the other men on her behalf as well as mine.

Thank you, Father, for Your healing hand in our grief.

The Calm Before the Storm

New Year's Day 1997 was another normal day near the end of a season of trouble-free years. Especially since 1991, when I'd launched into the career for which God had made me, Rosie and I had enjoyed smooth sailing with only a minor squall now and then. I was in my sixth year working full-time at Baptist Manor, and Rosie had a happily fulfilling job with the Red Cross. We were living in our custom-built Victorian dream home, and I was enjoying my dream car—a 1957 Chevy.

Rosie was at or near her ideal weight, enjoying the full bloom of health. New dreams and plans began to emerge. I could hardly wait to try jogging with Rosie, to go biking together, to swim together, and to outfit her with a beautiful new wardrobe of clothes.

Life just does not get much better than what we had.

On this leisurely January 1, I wrote in my journal, thanking God in advance "for the promise of Your help and presence with us and in us for each day of this new year." Before the year was out, we would need His help and presence as much as we ever had.

The year stretched on. In September I attended the Men's Roundup, an annual Labor Day weekend event at Oregon's Camp Tadmor. The main speaker, Steve Farrar, challenged me to "finish strong," continuing to accelerate spiritually in my walk with God until the end of my earthly life.

In mid-September I began attending a ten-week class at Western Seminary, taught by Dr. Englizian, called "Readings in Spiritual Classics." I recall one reading in particular entitled "Celebrate the Darkness," about the way that God uses the "dark" or difficult times in our lives to shape us according to the character of Jesus Christ. I wondered what dark times might be awaiting me.

On September 18, Rosie was scheduled to undergo surgery—a tummy tuck and hernia repair. I was in the habit of attending the Portland pastors' prayer group, and while driving to the meeting I was listening to Charles Stanley on the radio. His topic was unconditional surrender, and he raised the question, "What in your life are you are hanging on to that you may be unwilling to surrender to God?" I later wrote in my journal,

> I began thinking about Rosie and her surgery today, and probably another surgery in one more week. I struggled with whether or not I was willing to surrender her to God, and place her in His hands for *His* will to be done.
>
> During the prayer time with the pastors, You, Lord, kept bringing this to my mind. I felt You making it clear that I needed to decide. Finally, near the close of our prayer time, I shared this with the pastors. One of them suggested I sit on a chair in the middle of the circle. Many of them gathered around me and took turns praying for Rosie's surgeries to go well and for me to be able to surrender her to You, Lord. Thanks, Lord, for enabling me to pray out loud and surrender Rosie to You, and submit to Your perfect will. I was thankful that Bob Powell was there, kneeling in front of me. What a dear and loving and compassionate brother.
>
> I felt deep emotions and wept much as I seriously thought about the surrender and sacrifice I was making. I'll never forget hearing one of the pastors remark in his prayer and for my encouragement, "Remember the ram in the thicket."[7] Lord, what a powerful reminder of your loving provision for us when

---

[7] See Genesis 22:1-14, especially verse 13.

we are willing to sacrifice and surrender what you request. Before we prayed, I told my fellow pastors that Rosie is my most priceless treasure here on earth, and I could not imagine life without her.

Two weeks later, on October 2, I was reflecting on the poem "Footprints" by Margaret Fishback Powers, which I love so much. In my journal I wrote,

> I was reflecting upon that poem and the picture of You *carrying* me through the most difficult times in my life. Then I thought about my habit of journaling as part of my daily devotional time. I remembered that there have been some days, or weeks, or even months in which I did not write anything in my journal. At first I was regretting that and wishing I had been more consistent. . . . Suddenly the thought came to me that perhaps there was a specific reason why I did not write on some days. The visual picture that came to my mind was that on those most difficult days *You, Lord*, came alongside me, took away my pen and paper, and lifted me in Your arms to carry me!
>
> O Lord, thank You for the many times in my life that You have lifted me into Your all-powerful, all-loving arms and carried me. I thank You for Your faithfulness to walk beside me daily through life. Your love for me is so strongly evident when our two sets of footprints become one set of footprints, and they are Yours!

On October 8, Rosie had her second surgery, this one on her arms and upper legs. It went well and she stayed overnight at the hospital.

Five days later, Rosie attended Dr. Englizian's class with me. Martha Baker, Pastor Don's wife, was there and hardly recognized Rosie, she'd lost so much weight.

I recall sitting in the family room with Rosie on Saturday morning, October 18. We read some Scriptures together and shared some of our deep needs and desires. I told Rosie I was feeling stressed with such a hectic and demanding schedule at Baptist Manor. Although I thoroughly loved the job, I was working long hours and felt my work was seldom done. I needed wisdom on how to cut back. This was difficult to do. Even now, more than seventeen years later, I consider that ministry to be my favorite of all my jobs, before or since. I still wish it were possible for me to be the full-time chaplain there again, but they've gone out of business.

Rosie, recovering well from her surgeries, said she was very anxious to get back to working full-time at the Red Cross. She wanted us to pray that she'd be able to return within one or two weeks as planned, and that she'd be at full strength. We prayed together for both requests. We rejoiced in God's goodness, love, and presence in our lives. And we waited for Him to answer these prayers in the coming days.

Struck Down, but Not Destroyed

The next day, Sunday, October 19, 1997, we attended our adult Sunday school class together and then attended the ten forty-five worship service at Good Shepherd Community Church. Lead Pastor Stu Weber was preaching. To my surprise, Rosie, who usually preferred sitting in the middle or the back, said she wanted to sit in the front row. We enjoyed a delightful and encouraging time of worship with our church family.

Blessing upon blessing.

We returned happily home. That's when Rosie collapsed on the floor. I called 911. The firefighters arrived, followed soon by an ambulance, and they took Rosie away to the ER at Kaiser Sunnyside Hospital.

We soon learned she'd had a massive stroke. Her life was in danger.

Will she survive?

Will my beloved live to continue sharing my life?

Do the doctors know exactly what's happening?

Do the doctors know what's best for my wife?

Oh God! What's happening? Why, God, why? Oh, God, where are You?

In a moment, our lives were turned upside down. Our dreams shattered.

Time stood still!

Rosie lived. The next several months were so focused on the here-and-now, daily routine of fighting to regain her memories, her speech, the use of her right side, that the fuller implications of the situation didn't immediately sink in. Rosie spent three months in rehab, away from home. And I felt lost. Utterly unable to eat or sleep properly. It was too painful to eat alone. I was unable even to pray, except sometimes in agreement with someone else's prayer. Also I lost my ability to talk much for many weeks due to laryngitis, resulting from my severe, undiagnosed acid reflux.

God reduced me to sheer infancy. I was absolutely dependent on my Father. I couldn't rely on my experience as a chaplain or any other resource. All my usual props were knocked out from under me—especially Rosie, my strongest support.

During those early days, I was tense and fearful over the uncertainty about whether Rosie would live. And then how long it would take for her to recover. My hopes for a speedy recovery were dealt a sudden blow one day. I observed the speech therapist asking Rosie to point to different parts of her face. Rose would point to her eyes when asked to point to her ears, mistook her mouth for her nose, and so forth. That scared me and robbed me temporarily of hope I desperately needed.

And how would we survive financially with me having to be her primary care provider?

People would travel to be with me—just to be present, sometimes without saying a word. These were the people who really understood my need. Among these were a newly married couple who would soon become (and still are) two of our best friends—Kofi and Saundra Nelson. They prayed and spent time with both Rosie and me, listened to me, helped me pay bills, provided meals, and generally helped renew my hope. I felt loved and knew I wasn't alone.

Some people struggled to understand and assumed, "You deal with this every day as a chaplain. Where's your faith? Why aren't you trusting God?" Being misunderstood like that compounded my problem, deepened my sense of aloneness.

After Rosie returned home, I stayed busy taking her every week to see doctors and three therapists. God blessed Rosie with excellent care professionals, and all of them were amazed at her sweet, upbeat spirit. Progress was slow, but substantial.

Kofi and Saundra with us, shortly before Rosie's stroke

I spent as much time as possible with Rosie. I loved her as much as ever. But suddenly I felt I was married to a different person. Especially in the early weeks and months she experienced extensive memory loss, and her communication difficulties raised a barrier that we had never faced in twenty-two years of marriage. We had always shared everything at a deep level, and now words completely eluded her. It took months of therapy for Rosie to regain the semblance of a full vocabulary.

Once we got past merely existing in survival mode, we both began to come to terms with the radical differences and serious questions in our life. For a time well-wishers who assured me that a full recovery was only a matter of time kept my hopes up. But eventually the truth began to settle in: This wasn't temporary. Rosie was permanently disabled. And we began to put to rest many of the dreams we had begun to dream when Rosie had been losing weight. God could have healed her completely, but He chose not to, and adjusting to that was hard for both of us. Rosie couldn't work or drive. She had lost much of her independence and was much more isolated from people. But she kept her disappointment—perhaps even her grieving—to herself and didn't talk much about it to me or anyone else. Maybe she didn't know how to explain it. I think she had begun, in these difficult, dark days, to consider a sobering choice for taking control of her own future, and she wanted to keep power over this one decision.

150

We couldn't afford to hire anyone to care for Rosie. I wondered if I could return to the chaplaincy while providing the care that she needed. I did return, and Rosie even came with me sometimes.

I remember Don Baker, as he was finishing interviewing us for his book in 1984, saying, "Jerry, Rosie has stood by you and helped you overcome your biggest struggle. Now it's your turn to stand with her and help her overcome her biggest struggle." At the time he was referring to Rosie's struggle with her weight; little did we know that his words would later apply even more appropriately to *her struggle for her life.* As difficult as it sometimes has been, I love this woman so much and I'm so grateful to her that serving her in her time of need has been a genuine privilege and joy.

In Hawaii, one year after stroke

Conflict and Resolution

For a number of years leading up to summer 2000, I was increasingly sobered by the realization that only God's protection and grace rescued me from the homosexual lifestyle before AIDS arrived on the scene. Through my chaplaincy I was meeting more and more people with AIDS, and I was growing in love and compassion for them. I wanted to learn more about AIDS and to minister more effectively to those affected by it.

I had heard Chaplain Bob Walter of San Francisco General Hospital speak a few times at Baptist Manor. I learned that he supervised an eight-week hospital training course for HIV/AIDS ministry through his hospital. I applied and was accepted to take the training during June and July 2000. It was an excellent program, and I returned much better equipped for this aspect of my ministry.

While there, I had the special privilege of staying with Gary and Lynn Tuck. He had been a friend at Hinson and in seminary, from whom I took a year of piano lessons in 1974-1975. Besides being my favorite piano teacher, he was (and still is) a professor teaching at Western Seminary's San Jose campus. He even invited me to speak that summer to the student body about my life experience.

Gary and I both speak "Pianese"

Partway into my four hundred hours of clinical training I experienced an unexpected conflict with Sylvia (not her real name), who was a part of the hospital's chaplaincy program. Sylvia was also helping out as an instructor and discussion facilitator in my training. In one of the group sessions I opened up and shared my life story briefly. I spoke of my struggle with homosexuality and referred to it as an addiction. I shared how I came to realize I was a homosexual sex addict, and that I considered homosexual lusting and behaviors to be sinful in God's sight. I explained that I had found freedom from that lifestyle.

I knew that Sylvia was openly lesbian. Just a few days after that group session I learned that she had been deeply offended by what I had said. She could hardly believe that I would say such things in her and the other ministry interns' presence. I later learned that a number of the others present had been shocked and offended. I heard of this offense from Chaplain Bob Walter, my supervisor. He helped me understand what had happened and how my words were taken. Chaplain Bob understood and sympathized with my beliefs and testimony. Yet at the same time he was very concerned that that incident could cause a huge breach of trust and faith. He even said this might prevent me from completing the internship training.

Chaplain Bob encouraged me to talk with Sylvia and seek her forgiveness. I was very willing to atone for my unwitting offense. Bob then helped arrange a meeting that included Sylvia, another lady chaplaincy volunteer, Chaplain Bob, and myself. I suggested to Bob that it might be helpful for Sylvia and the other lady to read Don Baker's book about me. He passed along a copy to the ladies. But instead of helping, it seemed to make matters worse. The ladies were angry at my pastor and my church and my counselor and others who had all "made me feel wrong and guilty for being gay." They told me that I was born gay and that God had made me that way. They were sad and upset that various people were not understanding this and were trying to get me to change, when in their minds change is not possible.

I explained to Sylvia that I never intended to offend her. I acknowledged that some of what I'd said had been insensitive to her and others with beliefs different from mine. I asked her to forgive me and she hesitated. She said she could not so quickly brush it aside; she needed more time to think it over.

The four of us talked a bit further. I was feeling exhausted, discouraged, and confused by the interaction. Then as we stood to leave, I thanked Sylvia and the other lady for their time and willingness to meet. I instinctively reached to shake hands with Sylvia. *To my great surprise she opened both her arms wide and began hugging me.* We shared a prolonged, warm, healing hug. I sensed from Sylvia a genuine attempt to show me love, acceptance, and a beginning of forgiveness.

The situation brings to mind the common expressions, "Actions speak louder than words" and "We disagree, but we can agree to disagree agreeably." Sylvia and I showed through our actions that we accepted each other with respect in spite of our differences.

Right after the session, Chaplain Bob told me privately, "I'm so proud of you! I don't know when I have ever been so proud of anyone as I was of you just now." Bob later wrote in his lengthy final evaluation:

> Jerry met also with other staff members of Sojourn along with myself in order to clarify his belief and opinions about the subject of homosexuality. While this was undoubtedly the most challenging encounter for Jerry, his personal compassion, ability to clarify issues, and humble approach brought a change in the thinking of the staff who were able to embrace Jerry and his experience in a new and refreshing light.

"Now all things are of God, who has reconciled us to Himself through Jesus Christ, and has given us the ministry of reconciliation, that is, that God was in Christ reconciling the world to Himself, not imputing their trespasses to them, and has committed to us the word of reconciliation. Now then, we are ambassadors for Christ" (2 Corinthians 5:18-20).

Waiting to Happen

Sunday, November 16, 2003 seemed to me like the beginning of any other normal week. I didn't realize that this and many recent weeks had been tragically difficult for Rosie. In fact, Rosie's spirits had never fully recovered in the six years since her stroke.

She and I attended the worship service and our adult Sunday school class at Good Shepherd Community Church. After church we stopped to visit a friend we hadn't seen for several years, who was about to start chemotherapy.

The next day we both attended a memorial service for a twenty-eight-year-old woman who had committed suicide, leaving behind her husband, a son, and a daughter. We'd never met the young family, but we went to support the aunt of the husband, whom we knew.

Tuesday evening, after a full day of chaplaincy work, I arrived home, ate supper, told Rosie that I was very tired, and lay down for a three-hour nap. I got up just as Rosie was going to bed for the night. I was wide awake and alert, so I stayed up several hours and read before going back to bed.

About four o'clock Wednesday morning we both got up. Rosie said she had a splitting headache and needed some Tylenol. She asked me where some was. I told her we had a large container of it, but she said that she had taken all of it.

I did not realize at first what she meant, so I asked her about it. She told me she had swallowed all of her pills—including several prescriptions, such as her blood thinners!

"Why?" I asked in growing alarm.

She matter-of-factly stated, "I don't want to live anymore."

"What?" I sputtered, trying to grasp the situation. "Why?"

"Because nobody cares. Nobody really cares. Everyone is just too busy."

It suddenly struck me that my wife's life was in danger. By her own hand! I tried to stay calm and not panic. I kept noticing that Rosie had, as they say in the psychiatric field, very flat affect—that is, she appeared unemotional.

I told Rosie she needed to get to the hospital as soon as possible. She was not interested in going. I insisted. She resisted. Finally I called the hospital, and they said to bring her in immediately. If she refused to let me drive her, they told me to call 911. Then both police and an ambulance would come to take her in.

I reported the conversation to Rosie and once again asked her to go with me. She caught me off guard with her response: "But I haven't had any coffee yet." She meant it seriously.

I finally told her that if she would get dressed and gather some things to take with her, I would either fix coffee or get some on the way. With that she let me drive her to the hospital.

We arrived at Portland Adventist Medical Center a little before six and were in the emergency room for four hours, during which the doctors and nurses worked to save Rosie's life.

For the second time in our married life, I was a lost child—an infant, uncertain what to do or where to turn.

Later that morning, Rosie was admitted to one of the hospital psychiatric units. She spent three nights and four days in the hospital and returned home that Saturday.

For nearly a month I stayed with her, on high alert at all times. Neither of us was doing well. Shortly after coming home, she told me that she had decided she wanted to live after all. But she was not very forthcoming about her feelings and thoughts, and I couldn't be certain that she wouldn't make another suicide attempt. I tried to draw her out gradually, and learned eventually that she had been considering suicide for years—ever since her stroke and the far-reaching limitations on her life.

Constant vigilance took a terrible toll on my mental and physical health. One day Rosie took a fall and hit her head. I rushed her to the ER. The injury turned out not to be serious, and she wasn't admitted to the hospital. But I realized I wasn't ready for her to come home. To everyone's surprise I told Rosie and the ER doctor that I couldn't provide a safe environment for her, and I didn't want her to come home with me. A social worker helped us consider our options, and we ended up placing Rosie at Baptist Manor for several days, and then in a longer-term arrangement in a foster home. Insurance did not cover these stays, but I desperately needed the break, so we agreed to pay out of pocket. The foster home graciously allowed us to pay off their cost over the following years.

Finally Rosie was in a safe environment, and both of us had a chance to recover. She lived at the foster home for a month, through Christmas and into the new year, where God provided Rosie's spiritual therapy from an unexpected quarter. A young boy and girl lived in the foster home, and Rosie became especially attached to the little girl. Rosie would read to her new friend and play games with her. And the girl would run errands for Rosie. We began to refer to the girl as "God's little angel." She was the best medicine anyone could have given Rosie.

Interim Occupations

Rosie's suicide attempt shook me to the core. I found myself unable to perform my chaplaincy duties and went four months without working. Along with the gut-wrenching realization that I had almost lost my wife, I became heavily weighed down with a painful sense of my

156

own guilt. My thoughts kept racing to the conclusion that I was responsible for her loss of hope and decision to give up. If only I had been a better, more mature, more loving husband, then she would never have taken that drastic step. I kept on blaming myself and once again (as in the first three years of our marriage) believing that I was a total failure as her husband. It was not until I started meeting with a skilled and compassionate counselor that I finally came to understand and accept that I was not to blame for what Rosie chose to do.

In the midst of this adjustment process I found work selling cars at Gresham Toyota. While I wasn't the most effective salesman, I did enjoy constantly meeting new people. I had a natural ability to relate to people, to make them feel comfortable, as though I'd known them a long time. Unfortunately, this often backfired when the new relationship became the primary focus and buying a car became secondary.

I did sell a few cars though. One of my favorite sales came the day I noticed a Jaguar sedan on the used car lot and fell in love with it. I was enthusing about it to someone at the sales desk, and they responded, "Then you need to be the one to sell it!"

So I did. A man who seemed to have a good source of funding walked in looking for a used car. I showed him the Jaguar first, sharing my admiration for both the interior and exterior, but he said, "I'm not sure I want a Jaguar."

I talked him into a test drive. He ended up buying the car.

After one year the company had to let me go for inadequate sales. But they did it with regret. I remember my manager saying, "Jerry, I wish we could clone you," because of my people skills.

I went another few months without work, and then in fall 2005 I was hired by Costco, where I worked for two and a half years. I performed a variety of duties, including pushing carts in the parking lot—my least favorite task . . . unless seagulls were present. My favorite task, by far, was getting people to upgrade to "executive" memberships. I had freedom to do this inside or outside the store, and I could talk with anyone I wished, even in multiple languages! I did so well at this that my supervisor once echoed the words of my Gresham Toyota manager: "Jerry, I wish we could clone you."

As much as I enjoyed working at Costco, the job was physically demanding. I was in an eat-sleep-work cycle with little time for Rosie or ministry opportunities. Then came a moderate inheritance from Rosie's father, and I found myself wrestling for the next several weeks with the idea of quitting at Costco. Rosie wanted me to quit; she missed me. I talked several times with my manager, a believer in Jesus, hoping he would provide the answer. Finally, during one of our conversations, he said, "Jerry, I think you already know what you want to do."

"You're right," I admitted. "But it's scary."

It was the middle of a June night in 2008 when I woke up, still torn over the decision. *I really love Costco,* I prayed. *Especially the people.* Then suddenly the words sprang to mind: *But God, I love You more.*

That's when I realized that the provision through Rosie's inheritance was no accident. God was providing us an opportunity for a stress break, a chance to travel and enjoy each other without pressure. That's when I made my final decision.

The next day I said to Rosie, "Now I know I'm going to quit. But what will we do with our time and money?"

We agreed on one priority, no matter what else we did: I needed to finish the book I'd been working on for three years.

That was seven years ago.

Chapter 12

Recent Years

O LORD my God, I will give you thanks forever.

—King David, Psalm 30:12, NIV

But God, who called me here below,
Will be forever mine.

—John Newton, "Amazing Grace"

Even though Rosie and I left the leadership of Reconciliation Ministry in 1987, we have continued to receive referrals from people and churches who know our history. Not a year goes by that we don't have a handful of appointments and phone calls with people affected by homosexuality—either those struggling with same-sex attraction or their family or friends.

I remember one couple who met with us on a Saturday morning more than ten years ago, referred to us by a counselor. They had been married twenty-plus years and had a grown daughter and son. They were Christians and were active in their church.

He had just recently told his wife for the first time about his struggle with homosexual thoughts and feelings. He had never been involved in any sexual behavior with other men. His counselor had shared Don Baker's book about Rosie and me, so he and his wife had both read it.

Rosie and I thoroughly enjoyed our time with this delightful couple. As they shared, my heart ached for both of them as they searched for answers, understanding, and renewed hope for the future.

Unfortunately, I've learned since that the husband concluded he was, in his words, "living a lie." He left his wife and went into active homosexuality.

Not all of the stories in which we intervene go this direction, but many do. I can only trust that Rosie and I have at least some small impact for good in each situation.

Habits of the Heart

The first time I went to the hospital with severe chest pain was Tuesday, May 8, 2007. I felt weak and had difficulty thinking clearly. The ambulance came about six in the evening and took me to Mount Hood Medical Center in Gresham. The ER staff performed various tests and decided to admit me overnight. Meanwhile I stayed busy on the phone, updating family, friends, and a couple of churches and asking for prayer. I also kept in touch with Rosie, who couldn't drive because of her stroke.

I was awake Wednesday morning by six thirty and made some more phone calls. A little later my general practitioner came to check on me. Near the end of his visit he asked if there was anything unusual going on in my life. A bit sheepishly, I mentioned that I had been falling asleep while driving and one time at work while standing, waiting to talk to someone. My doctor sobered immediately and ordered me to stop driving and stop working until I could be tested for sleep apnea (blockage of the airway during sleep). That took some time to sink in.

"I have to drive," I protested. "Rosie can't drive. And I have to work, because we need the income."

In no uncertain terms, my doctor replied, "You are a hazard on the road, both to others and to yourself!"

That's when my denial broke and I acknowledged the truth. I ended up not driving for a whole month and was off work for just over a month.

Later that morning a cardiologist took me through a treadmill stress test to check the condition of my heart. He said I did excellent, and I felt great! I got up to 105 percent of the desired heart rate for my size and age, with no problematic symptoms.

The cardiologist reported, "Whatever problem brought you in here, it's obviously not your heart. Your heart is strong and in very good shape." He even added, "You'll never have a heart attack."

A few weeks later I had an overnight test in a sleep lab and found out that I did have severe sleep apnea. My sleep doctor prescribed a CPAP (constant positive air pressure) machine and told me that if I did not use the machine, I would put myself at much higher risk for heart attack or stroke. So I have used it regularly and I feel much better.

While the sleep measures have helped with my daytime fatigue, I have still experienced periodic episodes of chest pain and confusion, including a couple of times in the months prior to this writing. To the best of anyone's understanding these are stress-related; I guess I need to learn to relax more.

Pureheart Ministries

Throughout spring 2009 I attended the weekly Tuesday morning Men's High Ground gathering at Good Shepherd Community Church. One week the event featured the testimonies of the founders of Pureheart Ministries—a Christian organization established to help men struggling with sexual addictions. They offer individual counseling and mentoring, as well as weekly small groups for accountability and support. The founders, one of whom was Tim Davis, had both been pastors as well as sex addicts. Their openness and powerful testimonies began to convict my heart. I still struggled with keeping my thought life pure and with masturbation.

They handed out copies of a sexual activity survey. When I completed mine, my score definitely indicated the need to go in for a "Pureheart assessment." I delayed out of pride, but after a month I reluctantly called and spoke with Tim. We met for an assessment, after which Tim strongly suggested I could benefit from counseling. Tim was surprised that in my past counseling I had never dealt with some deeper issues, such as breaking "soul ties"—that is, spiritual connections with past sexual partners. He encouraged me that I could achieve a much deeper level of healing and freedom from sexual addiction, and he offered to counsel me.

"Jerry," Tim told me, knowing my love of seagulls, *"I see you like a seagull chained to the ground and unable to fly. One by one, God is cutting the chains, and one day you'll be able to soar as you were meant to."*

His comment has always reminded me of the fourth verse of the hymn "And Can It Be" by Charles Wesley:

161

Long my imprisoned spirit lay
Fast bound in sin and nature's night;
Thine eye diffused a quickening ray,
I woke, the dungeon flamed with light;
My chains fell off, my heart was free,
I rose, went forth, and followed Thee.

It was difficult and humbling to acknowledge my need for counseling. After all, I had started a ministry to help men and women struggling with same-sex attraction and had counseled a variety of people. My need raised questions in my mind. *Am I not already healed? Is this admitting that I have not been "completely healed"? What will people think? What will Rosie think? How can I explain this to Rosie?*

Thankfully, I finally humbled myself and put myself on the path toward consistent sexual purity—both in thoughts and actions.

I got weekly counseling from Tim for three years—and have found it very helpful and practical. One unexpected and refreshing benefit I experienced in my sessions with Tim was this: We did not always talk about my sexual temptations and failures. There were many times when the subject of sex did not even surface; rather we would talk about other deep areas of struggle in my life, such as understanding the major changes in my relationship with my beloved wife, Rosie. Both Rosie and I increasingly became aware of more and more changes in our daily lives resulting from her strokes and declining overall health.

Also, I have worked with a couple of other counselors since then, who have helped me identify and learn constructive ways to reduce my stress levels. I have also been attending a small weekly support group for the past six years. Both in the counseling sessions and in the small group we share many aspects of our lives with one another and do not merely talk about sexuality. The very specific questions we must each answer during weekly check-ins have provided strong accountability and a good deterrent to relapsing.

The M File

Writing about masturbation is embarrassing. But it's important enough that I feel compelled to overcome my reluctance for the sake of others.

Early on, Tim Davis asserted that if any man wants to break free from sexual addiction, he needs to stop masturbation completely. That was sobering and convicting to me.

Opinions differ regarding masturbation. Some people think it is always wrong and sinful. Others view it as an acceptable, normal part of life. Most of my life I fell somewhere in the middle. I believed it was wrong if accompanied by lustful thoughts, which are sinful. But I sensed it was okay if one could avoid lustful thoughts and simply masturbate for the sensation of pleasure and sexual release. I've more recently come to my own conclusion that, for me, all masturbation is wrong. You need to search the Scriptures for yourself and come to your own conclusion.

Most of my life I have masturbated. In my teens it was quite frequent, sometimes daily. Throughout the rest of my life it has been more sporadic, depending on my physical, emotional, mental, and spiritual condition. My parents did not talk with us kids about sex as I was growing up at home, and I did not feel comfortable asking questions. In fact, by the fifth grade or so I still did not know what caused pregnancy. I thought it had something to do with a man and woman being intimate, but I had no idea of the details.

My struggle with homosexuality was closely related to masturbation. During the time I was involved in homosexuality I felt that masturbation with another man was something I needed, and that it was not as bad as having sex with women outside of marriage. Since then the enemy has often deceived me into thinking that masturbating alone was "harmless" because it only involved me. In reality, masturbation is sexual expression done alone in perhaps the majority of cases. Some people have often described it as "solo sex." From the Bible I believe that God never intended for sex to be a solo behavior, but rather a beautiful expression of one's affections, exclusively between husband and wife in the marital relationship.

I was able to stop masturbating for an extended time in more recent years, which was most encouraging to me. At times I have been very encouraged and hopeful to be able to find complete victory, and other times I have felt it was hopeless. My increasing desire now is to completely stop this behavior.

My life is not about myself alone. I am not an island. All of my thoughts and actions may either immediately or eventually have their effects on others. I want my life to be a strong source of hope and encouragement to others and to be an example for others to follow.

Tim Davis recently told me, "Masturbation is a sin because of what you think about while doing it—lustful thoughts, pornographic material, previous sexual encounters and fantasies, and so forth—all of which the Bible states are sins." I personally agree with his definition. Tim went on to apply this to my life situation resulting from Rosie's physical limitations due to her strokes: "Jerry, you have double or triple the stress of the average man.... One of the major hurdles or challenges you have is that you are a married man who has had no sexual outlet for more than seventeen years. You are married, yet needing to live in a sense as if you were a single, celibate man."

One step I've taken to conquer all sexual sin has been to devise, under Tim's guidance, a "Purity Plan" for myself. Central to this plan is Romans 12:1-2: "I beseech you therefore, brethren, by the mercies of God, that you present your bodies a living a sacrifice, holy, acceptable to God, which is your reasonable service. And do not be conformed to this world, but be transformed by the renewing of your mind, that you may prove what is that good and acceptable and perfect will of God."

When I wrote up this plan in 2009, I had been living undisciplined and out of accountability. I realized I cannot be neutral and just go with the flow. I must become stronger and consistent in saying no to temptations and sin, and yes to obedience to God. So my plan included three lists:

- *Some things to which I am saying* no. This included, for me, masturbation, pornography, dwelling on past sinful experiences, watching movies that highlight sinful behaviors, and cultivating lustful thoughts toward others.
- *My game plan when tempted.* I worked up a few specific steps I would take when the enemy came knocking at my door, including immediate, honest prayer, calling someone else to ask for prayer, using Scripture, and using praise music.
- *Some things to which I am saying* yes. I wrote up specific goals (whats, wheres, whens, and hows) for personal devotions, for my relationship with Rosie, for exercise, for finishing my

autobiography, for my finances, for weekly counseling, and for Scripture memory.

The yes list is just as important as the no list. We can't just push sinful behaviors and thoughts out of our lives. We must *replace* them with positive behaviors and thoughts. Over time the natural reward of the positives will make them more and more attractive, and the sinful behaviors and thoughts will become less and less attractive.

Life's Greatest Certainty

You will show me the path of life:
In Your presence is fullness of joy;
At Your right hand are pleasures forevermore.
(Psalm 16:11)

Throughout my career as a chaplain I've encountered death at every turn. But never have I felt so surrounded and personally impacted by death as I have during the last ten years or so. As I've lived out my sixties, many of those I've known most intimately and counted on most heavily have died and left me behind.

I don't blame them. It hasn't been their fault. And for all the deceased who have known Jesus as Savior, I rejoice that they now see their Lord face to face and that I will join them one day.

But each time, I can't help feeling abandoned. Lately I've felt those particular losses very deeply. I think it has to do with my "three words"—love, listening, and presence. Each of these is so important to me, and they are connected with these precious individuals who have left me in the last ten years. Each of these people was someone that I knew loved me, and I loved them deeply in return. Now that they're gone, I can't love them in the tangible ways I used to; I'm lacking their presence and their ability to listen to me with compassionate acceptance. The loss, not only of the persons, but also what they have meant in my life has hurt me to the core. The pain of one loss fades with time, but it seems there is always another fresh loss to take its place, and I'm always having to adjust. More of my loved ones are going more and more quickly as the years pass.

My father died on August 15, 2005. At Dad's memorial service we remembered his work with gold and guns. We remembered his fishing and hunting. We remembered his poetry and his love for music. And his love for God. I played the piano prelude. We enjoyed "How Great Thou Art," "'Tis So Sweet to Trust in Jesus," and "It Is Well with My Soul." My brother, George, recited our father's life history and read some of his poetry. And various other friends and family shared their memories.

I deeply miss you, Dad, and increasingly realize the significant and lasting impact you had on my life. You and Mom gave me some of the greatest gifts possible: *You loved me unconditionally, you loved one another deeply, and you helped lead me into a personal and eternal relationship with Jesus Christ.* What more could I ever want?

In early November 2010 we lost Joel MacDonald. My heart sank and I tried to process this rearrangement of my life. I was unable to understand it at first, I suppose in part because I did not want to believe it. I had first met Joel in seminary in the early seventies, and we enjoyed a friendship of nearly forty years. Joel led our growth group at Hinson, and he counseled me for more than a year when I first "came out" to him and Don Baker.

Dr. Crosby Englizian went home to the Lord in early February 2012. I enjoyed his teaching on church history in seminary. He would start each class by sitting on the front of his desk and asking us, "How are you today? What's going on in your lives?" Then he would wait expectantly, with genuine concern, for our answers. But more than anything else I remember him as the man who listened to a broken, distraught, sinful student and loved him. I wish I could still talk with him on the days remaining of my journey, but I look forward to getting caught up on *that* day.

And my mother died on April 11, 2012. My friend, Pastor Tom Baker, came alongside us at that critical time of grief and officiated at Mom's memorial service. We remembered Mom's love for us, her family, throughout her life of nearly ninety-seven years. She was a teacher; first grade was her favorite. She enjoyed gardening, reading, and traveling. She loved the Lord. And I learned hospitality from my amazing mother. Again I played piano for a parent I'd just lost. George and I read poems by our father. And we enjoyed "You Are My Sunshine," "It Is Well with My Soul," and "'Tis So Sweet to Trust in Jesus."

For a considerable time before she died I was afraid that her death would be very difficult for me to accept. Yet, to my surprise, when she died, I did not cry much. I mentioned that to a cousin, and she suggested that it was because I had been saying good-bye to Mom over several years, due her memory loss from Alzheimer's.

Mom was a great listener. She was the one who encouraged me to pursue music. She prayed for me throughout my life. And I'll never forget that she was there when I overcame my greatest fear and shared about my past in front of a crowded church. I think of her often when I play the piano.

Losing Her by Degrees

Some losses aren't sudden and complete—sometimes they're partial and gradual.

Rosie and I had just returned a week earlier from a fantastic ten-day trip to Southern California. We'd gone by Amtrak and took Rosie's power chair with us. I attended the Health Care Ministry Association annual seminar, and we enjoyed Disneyland and the San Diego Zoo.

Then on Friday, May 14, 2010, after dinner we had a visit from one of the newer residents at Gresham Manor, where we were living. Soon after she left, Rosie got up from her recliner but could only stand. She was unable to walk. At first she thought her right leg had merely gone to sleep. I helped her into her power chair and into the bathroom. Soon we realized something was wrong. She was still unable to move her right leg. We called the on-call doctor, who told me to take Rosie to the emergency room. So we went to the Portland Adventist Medical Center, where Rosie spent three days and nights. She had had another stroke.

This was the third time I was confronted with the serious possibility of losing her through death. My thoughts quickly rushed back to her first stroke in 1997, when the doctor told me just three days or so after her stroke, *that she could have another stroke anytime and die.* That instilled an ongoing fear that God might choose to take her suddenly, without any warning. This realization has grown and remained with me to the present. As I have gradually processed this reality over the years, I know in a general sense that we are all in the same uncertain situation. We only live one day at a time, and never know for sure whether we will be alive the next day. But God intends us to live by faith and not by sight.

Hence, as I seek to place my faith and my very life in His all-powerful, all-loving hands, I have nothing to fear.

The human heart is forgetful. My fear creeps up on me often. And God reminds me—sometimes through difficult circumstances—of His constant presence and love (as He would again three years later). Each lesson is an opportunity to learn and grow. And trust.

Over the next two months, Rosie would occupy two rehab facilities and an assisted living facility before returning home. Meanwhile I was staying alone in our apartment at Gresham Manor.

Once again I was a basket case. I felt terrible in most every way—physically, mentally, emotionally, and spiritually. I felt pulled in different directions every day. My heart longed to stay with Rosie all day every day, to ensure that she received proper care. But I'd also neglected my own basic needs badly; I wasn't sleeping or eating well, and I didn't seem able to slow down and pray in order to reestablish peace. I felt so gloomy that I would turn on all the lights in the house in order to dispel the unbearable darkness.

Life had gotten out of control. That is to say, out of *our* control. Surely it is never out of the Lord's control. Remembering the Lord's benevolent sovereignty would always bring a small ray of comfort and hope to my weary soul. But never before had I realized how much I prefer being in control. I don't have a problem with change, but I want to be the one to make the changes. I wanted to control Rosie's condition. But instead I could only pray for her to be at peace and to know the Lord's presence moment by moment. I prayed for her to be filled with hope and peace and joy and purpose, which ultimately I was helpless to provide anyway. The Lord alone is omniscient, omnipotent, and omnipresent. (Once again, Kofi and Saundra Nelson stepped into the gap. They did so much more than say, "We'll pray." They *prayed* with us over and over in person and by phone, often reminding us of God's love and divine attributes. What refreshing lights in our days of darkness.)

Through these circumstances God forced me to give up my "right" to run our lives. I worked hard to acknowledge and submit to His loving lordship.

One of the bright spots in this difficult time was a phone conversation with my friend Willie. He likened me to George Bailey in *It's*

A Wonderful Life, meaning that I had impacted his life in ways that I didn't know.

"Jerry, you are definitely one of my heroes," he said. "Your life made a difference in my life. You're an unsung hero. I'm still alive today because of your influence in my life."

He reminded me to trust God no matter what.

I needed that reminder, I felt so confused, uncertain, alone. I felt like a drunken sailor aboard a ship in the midst of a terrible storm, trying to stay on his feet and survive.

Oh, Abba, I prayed on one occasion, *my beloved Rosie, my best friend, my faithful companion, my best listener, and my wife of almost thirty-five years is also in the midst of this storm. I miss her so much and I miss being together here in our home. I visit her several times a day, but that's not enough for her or for me.*

I needed to continue encouraging and helping Rosie through her difficult recovery. But I also needed Rosie's help and encouragement. We took what courage we could from our time together, walking on the facility grounds, admiring the flowers, or just sitting together in silence.

Rosie longed to get out of there and come home. It seemed like an eternity before she did.

Since Then

We went through it all again in early 2013, although no stroke was involved this time. Rosie visited the ER three times in January and was finally transferred to a skilled nursing facility for intensive therapies. Again she was working to recover use of her right leg, which has never fully returned. Also, she has only limited use of her right hand, arm, and shoulder. We are both grateful she can get around with her power chair, and is able to transfer herself to and from her power chair with the help of a transfer pole by her bed.

In late February we received approval for Medicaid, and Rosie was able to move into Avamere at Sandy, a nice assisted living facility near Portland. But by that time I was once again doing very poorly. I was becoming increasingly anxious about Rosie's situation and about having to live apart. I was not eating or sleeping well and was attempting to advocate for Rosie's needs constantly. Three times in eight days I was taken to the ER with temporary high blood pressure, confusion, dizziness, and weakness.

Finally I was able to move in with Rosie in mid-March, and things began to improve for both of us. We have a spacious two-bedroom apartment, including one for my office. A lot of pressure has been taken off my shoulders with caregivers available twenty-four hours to help with Rosie's needs.

I continue to serve as a part-time chaplain at four different facilities. And music is still my refuge in times of stress and my joy in times of peace. I often wake during the night and have difficulty getting back to sleep. Then I sit at my electronic piano (listening through headphones so I don't bother Rosie) and play praises to the Lord, sometimes improvising, sometimes flowing through my favorite hymns and praise choruses.

I think back over my life, and one of the major themes has to do with sexuality. We are designed by God as sexual beings, but my sexuality was warped and broken early in my life, and much of my story has involved the battle for purity and God's gradual transforming process. Even though I have fought against this obsession much of my life, now I can say that the obsession is gone, and I am learning to overcome temptations and past memories with God's Word, His presence, and His strength. I have been experiencing encouraging growth in my manhood and my ability to relate well with other men in a healthy and godly manner.

I can imagine God coming to me at some point in my early adulthood and spelling out a scenario for me:

Jerry, you are going to struggle mightily with sexual temptation, and you will fail. You will sink so deep that you will contemplate suicide. You will publicly proclaim your sin and My glory in your victory.

You will gain and lose a great job, your dream home, your dream car. You will almost lose your wife, and she will become permanently disabled. Several times you will feel as helpless as an infant, totally dependent on Me. You will be jobless, your wife will attempt suicide, you

*will be taken to the hospital numerous times, you will
have times of plenty and times when you are penniless.*

*I've planned all of this and more in advance. And
each time you feel most helpless and hopeless, I'm going
to provide for you. I will carry you and your beloved
Rosie in My arms.*

What do you think of this plan, Jerry?

I can't say whether I would accept or reject such a plan at the outset, but from my perspective now I know that it all turned out for my good and for God's glory. He is constantly preparing us for heaven. And although my sin is my responsibility alone—never planned by Him—He never wastes an experience. He works the miracle of bringing good out of evil.

When He and I look back, I hear Him saying, "Wasn't it during those darkest times that I carried you?"

The solo I sang forty years ago during our wedding—the "Wedding Prayer"—was oddly prophetic of our lives. Especially the line that asks for "strength in sorrow, want, or pain." Here in our later years I also recall,

And when Life's sun shall set beyond the hill,
May we go hand in hand, together still. [8]

In fact, Rosie's and my long and sometimes difficult experience gives us an advantage. We have a totally different perspective from many other people. I'm a more effective chaplain, not in spite of what we've gone through, but because of it. I understand suicidal people. I understand spouses in grief. And I'm coming to understand personal loss better and better.

Sex or Intimacy?

Our hardships have also brought me to a revolutionary new understanding of an old concept: intimacy.

In the first twenty-two years of our marriage, we were able to experience freely all the levels of intimacy, including sexual intimacy. For

---

[8] Fern Glasgow Dunlap, "Wedding Prayer," New York: G. Schirmer, 1965.

more than seventeen years now—since Rosie's first stroke in October 1997—we have had to be more intentional about identifying, pursuing and cultivating other avenues for ever-deepening intimacy between us.

Our culture assumes sexual intimacy to be the very deepest possible level of intimacy. And I believed that line of thinking for most of my life. Then when our circumstances suddenly and drastically changed, my thoughts and feelings and creativity began changing to accommodate our new physical limitations.

The good news—no, the wonderful and encouraging reality—is that God provides all the strength and grace I need to be obedient to Him and to be faithful to my loving wife. In the interest of transparency, I'm still "in process," like all believers, and my obedience is not perfect. But I am encouraged with my gradual progress.

As I draw closer and closer to God, and closer and closer to Rosie, I have been seeing and rejoicing in what God is accomplishing in us. Supernaturally, God has been continuing to grow and deepen our overall intimacy as husband and wife, without the typical sexual behaviors. After forty years of marriage we know each other very well. We love each other more and more. Yes, really. It's a warmth and security that is difficult to describe until you've experienced it. Naturally, we would love to be sexually intimate, but we realize and accept that that is not possible. We must even sleep in separate, single beds in separate rooms. I often miss being able to snuggle and talk and just enjoy being physically close to each other throughout the night.

But God's grace enters in where human desire comes up short. By God's grace our misfortune has worked out to our good fortune. As Rosie's primary caregiver, I have cut back to part-time work as a chaplain, and we share much more time together. I go with Rosie to all her medical appointments, and usually help out by speaking for her. Everywhere we go, we literally stop to smell the roses . . . and other flowering plants—one of Rosie's great passions. We enjoy gardening together in pots and beds on the long, spacious deck of our assisted living facility. We enjoy playing a wide variety of table games, ranging from Skip-Bo to Chickenfoot to Rummikub to Scrabble and so forth. We still socialize together with good friends. We have fun working on correspondence together. And we share several other interests and activities.

I love simply hanging out with my best friend!

And speaking of best friends, what could be better than spending time together with *both* of my best friends at the same time? I am speaking of God and Rosie. You see, Rosie and I have been spending intimate time together with God in conversational prayer, as well as in deep, desperate cries—as of a child—for our Father's listening ear and for His wisdom and for His infinite power. For more than forty years, since even before we married, Rosie and I have been discovering deeper and deeper intimacy with our Father through prayer, in times of joy and sorrow. The ever-increasing levels of intimacy Rosie and I now experience are based upon our times with our mutual Best Friend—God.

Finally, I am thankful that God has given both Rosie and me a sense of humor. This has definitely helped us get through and move beyond the difficult times. When Rosie and I argue and become upset with one another, I eventually leave the room to let us both cool down. Then later I poke my head out timidly and say something like, "Is it safe to come out yet, or are you still in attack mode?" If she sticks her tongue out at me, then I know she's doing better. We both laugh and move on with the day.

Audience of One

When I contrast my early life with my life now, another major theme is *motivation*. The primary motivation for my thoughts, words, and actions has changed dramatically. I used to look for some man to fulfill my deepest longings and needs, to fulfill me and to love me fully. I kept searching for true love that would satisfy me.

But now, instead of being consumed day and night with self-centered, sinful, lustful thoughts of sex with men, my primary motivation is to honor and please God. More and more I focus upon God's love for me, as well as my love for God and for other people. I want to respond to God's amazing love with obedience—not just in my sexuality, but in every area of my life. This is a continuation of the desire that first became compellingly clear to me when I memorized Philippians.

What a liberating, exciting discovery God has revealed to me—namely that God Himself is the One for whom I was created and for whom I was seeking so much of my life! Why was I blinded for so long to the truth that I can only find peace, joy, and fulfillment in Him through cultivating a growing and deepening relationship in submission to Him? Just as a baby is fully dependent on his or her parents, likewise I am utterly dependent on my heavenly Father—yes, even for my every breath.

As Randy Alcorn so often states in his books, we all were created for "one Person and one Place." *Jesus is the Person, and heaven is the Place!*

Part III
My Next Thirty-Five Million Years

Chapter 13

I Can Only Imagine

When we've been there ten thousand years,
Bright shining as the sun,
We've no less days to sing God's praise
Than when we'd first begun.

> —John Newton, "Amazing Grace"

Many times in my life I've thought I'd like to live to age one hundred or beyond. Today that's not such a strong desire. Rather, I'm striving to know God better and to follow His leading more closely day by day, as long as He gives me breath. I'm thankful that the Lord keeps motivating me to live more fully for Him and for the benefit of others. I do not wish to retire, but rather to remain as active as He enables me to be.

In July 2011 I wrote my own obituary. No, I wasn't expecting to die any time soon, but I thought it might be a healthy exercise. It was quite sobering, and I recommend it to anyone. It causes one to take a different perspective on his or her life, looking at it from deathbed backward. It can make you consider what the rest of your life needs to be like in order for people to say the kinds of things you wish they would say in your eulogy. I'm more grateful now for each new day of life that God gives me here.

The Rest of My Story

I believe I still have a lot more to do here on earth. I can lead people to Christ and help them grow in their faith. I still have opportunities to earn eternal rewards, which God has prepared to be enjoyed in heaven. In my thoughts, speech, and actions, I can still be transformed further into the image of Jesus Christ. I want to keep on growing in knowledge of God and in obedience to Him. And I want to help others do the same.

For believers, life on earth is a process of *becoming* (growing, changing, sanctification). Life in heaven is a way of *being* (glorified, fully conformed to the image of Jesus Christ). I know this is an oversimplification, but it's helpful to me.

It's difficult for me to imagine what it will be like to live forever. I have thought about it many times but always ultimately come to find it mystifying and incomprehensible, yet by faith believable. I look forward to living in a perfect environment. In heaven there will be no sin, no Satan, no demons, no death, no pain, no illnesses, no sorrow, no aging. No more bills or financial struggles, no poverty, no dementia or Alzheimer's, no strokes, no heart attacks, no cancer. No need for doctors, nurses, hospitals, or jails. No hopelessness, no depression, no worries or fears.

In sharp contrast to the above incomplete list, there *will be* countless people and wonderful things present in heaven forever. The most important and marvelous truth about heaven is that it is God's home and we, as believers in Jesus, will share His home forever! We will see Jesus face to face. I can hardly wait to thank Him and worship Him in that glorious setting.

I'm also looking forward to the other company I'll be able to keep. Rosie has often said to me, "I know there are no marriages in heaven, but I've already reserved the cottage next door to you." What a compliment and blessing! I'd think she'd be tired of me by then. But I love Rosie so much that I want to live next door to her also.

Rosie and I both love having guests in our home. Just think of the dinner parties we'll be able to host. I can hear Rosie saying she'll cook the meal if I will set the table and help with the dishes. I look forward to meeting people from all over the world.

I can hardly wait to see Rosie in her new resurrected body. She will be whole and healthier than ever before. No handicaps and no limitations from strokes. The thought makes me weep.

And the opportunities to learn new things! In heaven I believe we will have an endless supply of books to read, with new ones being written throughout eternity. Heaven's library will make our US Library of Congress look like a child's bookshelf.

Both Rosie and I love to travel, to visit people, to see the sights, to enjoy God's creation. Then, we will not be limited by lack of money or time or good health. One of our former pastors said he thinks that in heaven we may be able *to travel at the speed of thought!*

And the reunions! Of course, I want to see and talk with Jesus most of all. But also our unborn child (or twins), whom we lost through miscarriage. And my parents and various relatives who trusted Jesus. (I wish I could have been there for the reunion of my mom and Aunt Vida, the twin sisters.) Our niece, Malana, who died at age twelve of leukemia. Dr. Vance Webster, my childhood pastor, on whose watch I placed my faith in Christ. Al Wilson, whose challenge to memorize Philippians changed the course of my life. And Bud Hinkson, and Joel MacDonald, and Chaplain Tim Malyon, and Dr. Crosby Englizian, and Dr. Earl Radmacher. And so many more.

And that's not to mention people mentioned in the Bible—David, Adam and Eve, Moses, Joshua, Paul, Lazarus, Mary and Joseph, the thief on the cross, Enoch, Noah, Abraham, John, Peter, and the other original disciples of Jesus.

And what about music in heaven? I'm hoping there will be pianos, and that I can take more lessons from Gary Tuck to improve my playing skills and compose new songs. I imagine that people who are not musical on earth may be able to sing or play an instrument beautifully in heaven. How exciting to hear the angels singing as they lift their voices in worship of God.

I look forward to being completely set free from sin. Free from temptations, from the affects of sin, such as guilt, shame, hopelessness, and the endless, repeating cycles I've experienced on earth. Yes, I will be set completely free forever from all sinful sexual temptations, lusts, fantasies, behaviors, and memories—both homosexual and heterosexual.

"Therefore, my beloved brethren, be steadfast, immovable, always abounding in the work of the Lord, knowing that your labor is not in vain in the Lord" (1 Corinthians 15:58).

"For our citizenship is in heaven, from which we also eagerly wait for the Savior, the Lord Jesus Christ, who will transform our lowly body that it may be conformed to His glorious body, according to the working by which He is able even to subdue all things to Himself" (Philippians 3:20-21).

I can hardly wait to be with the Person for whom I was created—Jesus—and to live in the home He has prepared—heaven!

Mining For Gold

Gold is valued and utilized in numerous ways. Countless people have risked their lives to find gold. Our nation once used the gold standard; our money was backed by the enormous stockpile of gold bullion stored securely at Fort Knox. Individuals and nations the world over value gold highly.

My father was a goldsmith for seventy years, yet my Father has been a Goldsmith all of His life . . . which, by the way, has no beginning and no end. He loves us so much He has prepared us an eternal city with streets of gold.

He and He alone is the Gold Standard of eternity—our God, as made visible in Jesus Christ, the God-Man. He is the most valuable One in eternity!

So let's keep on mining for gold, so that you and I will know better and better the Creator of all the world's gold and of all heaven's "gold."

Lord, my thoughts about heaven and my whole life on earth are like an unfinished symphony that will never be finished, on earth or in heaven. They are as endless as You.

Lord, please complete and polish my life into a life of gold, which will reflect the beauty of Your Son, Jesus Christ, who lives in me.

* * *

Wait! Do you hear what I hear? It sounds like heaven's glorious Grand Symphony Orchestra tuning their instruments and practicing their music. Not just any music, rather music for the great wedding of the ages, the marriage supper of the Lamb. Jesus, the Bridegroom, and the Bride (the body of Christ, the Church) will be forever united in love.

I can almost hear the angels with their pure voices, joining softly together as they rehearse with the orchestra. What fun! What joy! To dream about the deaf and the blind hearing and seeing this endless spectacle, perhaps singing together Handel's *Messiah,* especially the majestic, triumphant "Hallelujah Chorus."

The Lamb, the Lion of the tribe of Judah, the great Yahweh, the Creator, the Messiah, the Prince of Peace, the Good Shepherd, the Savior of the world, the King of kings, and Lord of lords is opening His mouth and continues rejoicing over His Bride with singing (see Zephaniah 3:17).

"Let everything that has breath, praise the LORD. Praise the LORD" (Psalm 150:6).

POSTLUDE

Be Still, My Soul (2015)

As usual, early in my devotional time I choose a hymn for the day. Today I settle on "Be Still, My Soul." I play it on the piano and sing the words quietly to myself. In particular, the third and final verse speaks to me:

> Be still, my soul: The hour is hast'ning on
> When we shall be forever with the Lord,
> When disappointment, grief, and fear are gone,
> Sorrow forgot, love's purest joys restored.
> Be still, my soul: When change and tears are past,
> All safe and blessed we shall meet at last.[9]

Afterward, I speculate in my journal why the Lord may have directed my focus to this hymn. I must need the words and message to start off my day. Only He knows what I will experience over the coming hours.

Then something unexpected, unusual, and yet refreshingly encouraging begins to take place as I continue writing my thoughts:

> Lord, I do not understand. How on earth, did You do that? How could You possibly take the turmoil, the stress, the fears from my soul, and replace them with a peace that surpasses all comprehension?

---

[9] Katharina von Schlegel, translated by Jane Borthwick, "Be Still, My Soul."

I can almost hear You whispering to me: *My son, you cannot fully comprehend the answer to that just yet. However, when you are living with Me in My Home, I will gradually reveal that answer to you, along with answers to many more of the countless questions you now have. Until then, my son, simply rest in My loving arms as I once again sing My love song over you. Enjoy the peace that I, and only I, can give you, for remember this truth, that I AM the Prince of Peace. Shalom.*

As I finish writing the last word, my tears start to slowly drip, then flow from my eyes. For I begin to realize that this has not merely been pen on paper. Rather, it has been God's heart to my heart. Yes, even to the depths of my innermost being.

What can I possibly say in response to this love He continually showers upon me? All I can say is: *Thank You, Lord, and I love You, in response to Your love.*

Thank You for being there.

Thank You for loving me enough to listen.

Appendix

Ministry Contacts

I gladly recommend each of these ministries, with which I am personally familiar. Feel free also to visit my website (JerryHeacock.com), where I will periodically update this list and the contact information.

Portland Fellowship
Jason Thompson, Executive Director
(503) 235-6364
PO Box 14841
Portland, OR 97293
Website: www.PortlandFellowship.com
www.TakingBackGround.com (mentoring program for adults)
www.ReachTruth.com (mentoring program for youth)
www.PortlandFellowship.com/hope (support program for family and friends)

This is the ministry Rosie and I started in 1980 in Portland, Oregon, originally known as Reconciliation Ministry. Phil Hobizal was my successor as director, followed by Jason Thompson.

Restored Hope Network
Anne Paulk, Executive Director
(503) 927-0869
PO Box 22281

Milwaukie, OR 97269
E-mail: office@RestoredHopeNetwork.org
Website: www.RestoredHopeNetwork.org

Mission Statement: "Restored Hope is an interdenominational membership governed network dedicated to restoring hope to those broken by sexual and relational sin, especially those impacted by homosexuality. We proclaim that Jesus Christ has life-changing power for all who submit to Christ as Lord; we also seek to equip His church to impart that transformation."

Pureheart Ministries
Tim Davis, MA, MDiv, Founder and Director
E-mail: tim@PureheartMinistries.net
Website: www.PureheartMinistries.net

This ministry provides pastoral counseling via skype and phone for men, women, and couples struggling with the impact of sexual addiction. They typically focus on counseling heterosexuals, but also counsel those struggling with bisexuality.

Eternal Perspective Ministries
Dr. Randy Alcorn, Founder and Director
(503) 668-5200
39085 Pioneer Blvd, Suite 206
Sandy, OR 97055
E-mail: info@epm.org
Website: www.epm.org

This is a nonprofit ministry devoted to promoting an eternal viewpoint and drawing attention to people in special need of advocacy and help. Randy Alcorn is the author of more than twenty books, with well over one million in print. See some of Randy's books in my list of recommended reading.

Appendix

Bible References

My favorite Bible verse: "For nothing is impossible with God"
(Luke 1:37, NIV).

This verse can be interpreted two ways: (1) God can do all things. In this interpretation the main subject and focus is God Himself. (2) A believer can do anything with God's help (see also Philippians 4:13, "I can do all things through Christ who strengthens me").

Personally, I believe the primary meaning in the context of Luke 1 is the first viewpoint. Just as God could make a virgin pregnant, He is able to do anything He chooses in your life and mine. In particular, He is able and willing to keep His every promise to us.

My favorite Bible chapter: Psalm 30, NIV.
This psalm describes in poetic form the story of my life. The repeated themes of sadness and joy, weeping and rejoicing pervade this powerful and inspiring psalm. God has removed my sackcloth and clothed me with joy. Therefore I want to give Him thanks forever. I memorized this psalm many years ago, and continue to recite it and meditate on it often. I can hardly wait to talk in heaven with David, the author, and thank him for writing it.

My favorite Bible book: Philippians—especially 1:6,21; 2:1-14; 3:17-21; 4:4-13.
God used this short book to help change my life, as I describe near the end of chapter 6 in this autobiography. By the time I had memorized about half of Philippians, God was overwhelming me with His love in new and powerful ways. I was especially struck with Jesus' profound expression of love-in-action in 2:5-11.

I also love many other portions of Scripture, and I encourage you to keep on searching the Scriptures to keep getting a fuller understanding of who God is and what He does. Read all sixty-six books of the Bible and keep reading them, studying them, and inviting God's Spirit to apply them to your life.

Appendix

Recommended Reading

My favorite book is the Bible, and my favorite translation now is the New King James Version. I recall what an elderly, godly man wrote in the front cover of a Bible he gave me in my youth, "Sin will keep you from God's Word, but God's Word will keep you from sin." Jesus said to Satan, when tempted in the wilderness, "Man shall not live by bread alone, but by every word that proceeds from the mouth of God" (Matthew 4:4).

After the Bible, the following are five books at the top of my current list:

A.W. Tozer, *The Knowledge of the Holy*. This is an excellent classic, a concise book dealing with the attributes of God. Tozer writes, "What comes into our minds when we think about God is the most important thing about us."

Eleanor H. Porter, *Just David*. This novel was my father's favorite book, and it is one of mine also. My dad kept loaning out copies of it to others. In the back of one copy he attached a note from one of his borrowers, reading, "If I could have just one book, besides my Bible, this would be it. It made me so sad with longing for the innocence lost in children today—and yet gave me hope. . . . Music is a language that touches people where nothing else can."

Taylor Caldwell, *The Listener*. I first read this book while living in Germany, serving in the US Army. The first time I read it, I cried through most every chapter. I kept on asking myself, "Is there actually someone like that, who will truly listen?"

Eric Metaxas, *Amazing Grace: William Wilberforce and the Heroic Campaign to End Slavery*. This is a powerful, well-written biography. The book and movie by this title were released at the same time.

Randy Alcorn, *Heaven*. This is the most complete and creative book on the subject of heaven that I have ever seen, an excellent resource for home or office. Just over five hundred pages, it includes a helpful variety of indexes and appendices, along with a question-and-answer format throughout. My copy is filled with post-it notes and highlighted portions.

Books Dealing with Sexuality
Randy Alcorn, *The Purity Principle*
Don Baker, *Beyond Rejection*
Andrew Comiskey, *Strength in Weakness*
Bob Davies and Lori Rentzel, *Coming Out of Homosexuality*
T.A. Davis, *Basic Training,* Phases One and Two
David Kyle Foster, *Love Hunger*
Dennis Jernigan, *Giant Killers*
Barbara Johnson, *Where Does a Mother Go to Resign?*
Anita Worthen and Bob Davies, *Someone I Love Is Gay*
Frank Worthen, *Destiny Bridge*

Other Great Books
Randy Alcorn, *The Grace and Truth Paradox*
Randy Alcorn, *Lord Foulgrin's Letters*
Randy Alcorn, *Seeing the Unseen*
Randy Alcorn, *The Treasure Principle*
Neil T. Anderson, *Victory over the Darkness*
Tom Baker, *Incarnation*
Ben Carson, *Take the Risk*
Fanny Crosby, *An Autobiography*

Patrick Kavanaugh, *The Spiritual Lives of Great Composers*
Margaret Fishback Powers, *Footprints*
Earl D. Radmacher, *You and Your Thoughts*
Earl D. Radmacher, *Salvation*
John Sloan, *The Barnabas Way*

Author's Thank You Notes

The first time I ever heard the powerfully moving song, "Thank You for Giving to the Lord," sung by William Harness, it stirred my imagination. It reminded me of the potential joy that is shared through a simple, sincere thank you. Fear not! I am not going to sing my thank yous. Rather, I will attempt to share them through inadequate but heartfelt words.

I love each and every person who has shared their love with me, whether for a short or a long period of time. I wish it were possible for me to mention every one of you by name, yet that is not possible. I pray that God will bless each of you and reveal Himself to you more each day in unexpected ways. But I do want to specifically thank a few:

First, I want to thank You, God, for creating me in Your own image, along with every person who was ever born. I thank You for drawing me into a personal relationship with Yourself while I was very young. I am grateful that You kept on loving me unconditionally during those many years I was living like a prodigal son. I am thankful that You forgave me all my sin and restored my hope when I felt hopeless and helpless. I thank You, Lord, for trusting me with the ministry of sharing Your love, comfort, forgiveness, and joy with others, of all ages. Thank You finally, Lord, for Your promise to take me to live with You forever in Your Home.

Second, Rosie, my wife, truly the love of my life. I thank you for choosing me to be your life partner. You did not know in advance how dark my life would become for awhile. Nor did you know how and when God would draw me up out of the pit and begin to set me free. Free to love Him and to love you and to love others as He had commanded me. You, with God's help, never walked away; you never gave up on me. Even though I so often wanted to give up on myself, feeling there was no good in me. We have fought some fierce battles together against the enemy of our souls. We are still together and still loving each other because God has walked with us, behind us, before us—and when we were too weak to walk any further, He picked us up together in His loving arms and carried us. As He held us each time, He would once again sing His love song over us. He would fill our hearts and minds with peace, then we would fall asleep in His embrace.

Third, Dan Britts has not taught me, but rather demonstrated to me what a true friend is like. I am eternally grateful to our heavenly Father for causing our paths to cross on the side of a hill called Mt. Tabor at such a pivotal time in my life. It was a test of faith for each of us for totally different reasons. Perhaps God was testing your willingness to obey what Jesus called the second-greatest commandment—namely to love your neighbor as yourself. I was your neighbor and you chose to love me with God's help and guidance. It is a mystery to me to this day why you were willing to love me as deeply, patiently, and consistently as you did. I do not think I could ever have loved you as you have loved me these past forty-four years, if the circumstances were reversed. Thank you for running up and down and around Mt. Tabor with me countless times. I only wish we could have run a marathon together. Yet you told me recently that finishing this book is far more important than literally running a marathon foot race! Thanks, Dan, for that word of encouragement.

Finally, I want to give a big hug and a hearty thanks to my editor and author coach, Brian Smith. As I have often asked you, "Where were you the first nine years I worked on this book?" I needed an editor, yet I needed far more. I needed someone skilled to coach me in the overall remaining process. I have heard of coaches in sports, but not coaches for authors. In God's wise timing He brought us together. Thanks, Brian, for your almost unbelievable patience with me in these nine months of teamwork. I was honored that you felt comfortable being so transparent with me from the start. You helped draw out my creative thinking and writing skills. With your surgical skills you cut out the unnecessary parts that would hinder the natural flow of my life's story. You questioned, challenged, inspired, encouraged, yet did not force your preferences upon me. I am thankful to consider you a new friend. May God bless you now and forever as a reward for your part in bringing my autobiography to completion.

About the Author

*J*erry Heacock earned his BA degree from the University of Oregon, majoring in German. He loves languages and thoroughly delights in using them whenever given the chance. Jerry served four years active duty in the Army directly after college, the last three years served in West Germany. His postgraduate work in preparation for vocational ministry was done at Western Seminary in Portland, Oregon. He graduated with an MDiv degree (master of divinity) in 1981, with a pastoral major.

Jerry has worked in a broad variety of jobs, including summer farm work in Texas, insurance sales with various major companies, delivering mail on a walking route, selling cars, working at Costco, and finally as a self-employed chaplain in a variety of care facilities for more than twenty years.

He is an avid music lover, especially fond of hymns, praise choruses, various Broadway musical scores, and classical music (including various operas). His favorite hymn is "Amazing Grace" and his favorite opera is *Fidelio* (the only one Beethoven composed). His favorite all-time movie is *Ben-Hur* and favorite musical: *The Sound of Music.* He has played numerous instruments, but his favorite is the piano.

Jerry loves traveling, reading, getting to know new people, running, writing, and most of all striving to grow in his relationship with God, that he may be better equipped to serve others.

He lives in Sandy, Oregon, with Rosie, his wife of forty years. In his words she is "the love of my life, my soul mate, and my best friend." They have no living children, but they by faith believe they have identical twins waiting for them in heaven.

Jerry may be contacted through his website: JerryHeacock.com